Wings

DISTINGUISHED STUDENT ESSAYS

17th Edition

From the Freshman Composition Program at California State University, Northridge

Dina Abdel Hady | Andzhela Keshishyan | Margeaux Aegel Gamboa | Nareen Manoukian

Printed in the United States of America

10 9 8 7 6 5 4 3 2 1

ISBN 978-0-7380-3897-1

Hayden-McNeil Publishing
14903 Pilot Drive
Plymouth, MI 48170
www.hmpublishing.com

Bourgeois 3897-1 F10

TABLE OF CONTENTS

LETTER FROM THE EDITORS

Congratulations on purchasing a copy of *Wings*. What you are currently holding in your hands is a collection of the best of the best pieces written by English 155 students. We took great care in choosing a diverse group of works that would be assigned to you in your composition class and we hope that you find these texts helpful.

The aim behind this book is to inspire, motivate, and educate our composition students. These works were published by your peers, former 155 students that you could run into in your stay with us here at California State University, Northridge. Because they are your peers, we want to emphasize the importance of dialogues and community. Thus, we included critical thinking questions to allow you to engage with these works.

These essays are wonderful efforts in terms of critical thinking, argumentation, and creativity; however, we also want you to know that you are part of this community as well. Your words and works are of importance to your instructors, their colleagues, your peers, and future 155 students. So, enjoy this book, spread your wings, and submit a copy of your best work at the end of the semester.

Sincerely,

Dina Abdel Hady
Andzhela Keshishyan
Wings *Editors*

Margeaux Aegel Gamboa
Nareen Manoukian
Wings *Assistant Editors*

ACKNOWLEDGMENTS

Wings would not be possible without the contribution and collaboration of many dedicated individuals. First, we'd like to thank Dr. Irene Clark, professor and director of the Composition Program, who has offered her invaluable expertise and support throughout this process. We would also like to express our appreciation to Dr. Pamela Bourgeois for her endless encouragement. Thank you to all English 155 instructors who help motivate students in developing and progressing as writers. Specifically, we would like to thank those instructors who devoted their time and energy to attend the readings and participate in the selection of these essays. A special thanks to the wonderful office staff in the English Department who have assisted with the numerous administrative tasks. An extended appreciation to Martha Alzamora, Karin Castillo, Tonie Mangum, Marjie Seagoe, Kavi Bowerman, and Eve Green. The tutors at the Learning Resource Center have also played a crucial role in the efforts to guide and support student writing. To Andrea Kinney and her talented team at Hayden-McNeil for their patient assistance—thank you for making the publication process fun! Last, but certainly not least, we would like to thank all of the English 155 students who submitted their work. Without you, this publication would not be possible.

A GUIDE TO USING *WINGS*

"Wings is fly."

—ASHLYN MORSE

ANNOTATED ESSAY
Adrianna Saavedra

Instructor: Terri Silverberg

Attention-grabbing title

WOULD YOU LIKE OBESITY WITH THAT?

One of the reasons why many people go off their diets and gain weight is because of fast food. According to Yves Engler, author of "The Obesity Epidemic: The Business Opportunities in Obesity," the rate of obesity has doubled in the United States since 1990. One in every four adults is overweight and 300 million people are obese." Obesity is one of today's biggest health crises, yet fast food corporations sell unhealthy food at a cheap price and encourage people to buy their food through misleading advertisements. Some people believe that consumers are responsible for their own weight gain because they choose to eat excessively at fast food restaurants. However, fast food franchises should be liable for obesity in the United States because they are aware of the unhealthy foods they provide customers, and use deceiving marketing strategies to sell their products.

Fast food corporations do not provide nutritious foods in their restaurants, even when they say they do. Michele Simon, founder and director of the Center for Informed Food Choices, reveals that the Physicians Committee for Responsible Medicine performed a nutritional analysis in 2003 on all the corporation's salad entrees with the result that "one of McDonald's salads was among the worst offenders having as many calories and grams of fat as a Big Mac" (Simon). Nobody could feel better after eating that salad instead of the Big Mac. Any corporation that sells salads should make them healthier than other items on the menu because people are trying to live healthier but still want to eat at their favorite restaurant and assume the salads have fewer calories. Salads are healthy products and give consumers the option of eating better, but they should actually be healthier with a low calorie dressing. Corporations such as McDonald's, Wendy's, Jack in the Box and others are trying to provide healthy options. However, they should not advertise their meals as "healthy" if they are not any better than a fast food burger. People are trying to improve their diets and with many being obese, salads or other wholesome options are a necessity. However, if the fast food corporations continue to advertise their high calorie and fat products as new healthy foods, obese people will not improve their health.

Some people argue that fast food franchises are improving their menus. According to Todd G. Buchholz, an economic advisor who served as the director of economic policy under President Bush stated, "Wendy's, traditionally known for its square-shaped hamburgers, offers a low-fat chili dish that the Minnesota attorney general's office recommended as a 'healthier choice' in its fast food guide." Many restaurants are improving because people want healthier meals. When the Physicians Committee for Responsible Medicine did an analysis of the salads, all the corporations had chicken in their salad entrees, which contains as much cholesterol as beef (Buchholz). However, most companies have now changed their salads and offer the option of no chicken (Simon). After the analysis of the salads, the restaurants improved their salads, which was a relief to many customers.

McDonald's is attempting to provide healthier meals for their customers. Mary Dillon who is responsible for McDonald's global marketing strategy, brand development, and the company's Balanced, Active Lifestyles initiative explains that, "McDonald's is motivating people everywhere to eat healthier and to make exercise a regular part of their lifestyle" (Simon). In spite of this, brand name companies such as McDonald's can be guilty of causing the "halo effect." This happens when a consumer believes that the company is selling "healthy" food and promoting active lifestyles; therefore, the consumer believes they are a good company. Fast food corporations are a business and they can be very successful through advertising. However, they should be more concerned about the health of their customers, instead of just trying to make their company "look good."

> Going back to the argument, refuting aspects of the counterargument

Fast food companies should be liable for obesity because they have deceptive marketing strategies. They often target children because they know how much children influence their parent's decisions. Marion Nestle, author of "The Fast Food Industry Intentionally Markets Unhealthy Foods to Children," explains how, "Fast food companies view school-children as an unparalleled marketing opportunity." Most American children attend school and this is the easiest way fast food corporations can target them. Marion Nestle explains that, "McDonald's offers cups, toys, placemats, movie coupons, special toys and mugs, and logo-labeled items for holidays, birthdays, and celebrations, and it does so in its outlets throughout the world" (Nestle). Fast food corporations use the schools to advertise their company. They use their own logos on school supplies or give away coupons to come to their restaurant. In their meals, fast food restaurants use recognizable figures, toys, and playhouses to attract children. Yves Engler states, "Of 10,000 children surveyed, 100 percent of U.S. children recognized Ronald McDonald." Ronald McDonald is a clown character used as a mascot for McDonalds. He is widely recognizable because of his energy, his clown costume, and his love for children. Because of him, children want to eat there. McDonald's is a fun place for small children because their "kid's meals" come with a toy. McDonald's also has playhouses where children can play and have fun while they eat. Children are the easiest to persuade, so getting them interested first brings in business from their parents.

> Going back to argument and linking back to the thesis

> Leading into quote

Fast food corporations also sell their products at a low price to attract people who need to save money. Their commercials are often geared towards low-income people. These corporations know that many people are not able to spend much money when they go out to eat. The fact that "nearly a third of the population is obese and two-thirds overweight, with the rates substantially higher among the poor" is appalling, but not surprising (Engler). Poor people are more likely to eat at a fast food restaurant because of the prices. Fast food is cheap, which is the best solution for low-income families because they are probably not able to buy expensive groceries and cook at home. Fast food companies also sell "bigger" food. Studies have shown that "people consume about 30 percent more when served larger portions" (Engler). Corporations are selling more for less and advertising "bigger as better," which is more likely to cause people to overeat.

> Topic sentence connects this paragraph with the one before

Some people believe that fast food franchises should not be liable for obesity because the nutrition guides are available on the fast food restaurants' websites. It is true that these companies do not hide anything from the consumers. However, not all people read the

Addressing counterargument, agreeing to an extent but then linking back to argument

nutrition guides because they do not have the time to search the facts about everything they eat and some may not understand it. Does everyone actually search a restaurant's website for nutritional facts? Not many people have the time to view all the details about what they are eating. Does everybody in the United States own a computer? To view these nutritional facts, people need an Internet connection, and not everyone is able to afford it. Although McDonald's restaurants do provide their nutrition facts on the walls of their restaurant, all fast food corporations should place their nutrition facts on the walls, on their menus beside the meal, or on the wrappers of the products.

The biggest argument against holding fast food corporations liable for obesity is that consumers have a responsibility to be cautious about what they consume. Eating fast food is not a crime and can be eaten without problems as long as people do not abuse their consumption. People have to control themselves to only eat fast food occasionally. According to an interview on the Obesity Policy Report, Radley Balko, a policy analyst for the libertarian Cato Institute, states, "If consumers truly want healthier options, they'll indicate that preference by buying healthy" (Balko). For example, consumers have a choice to ask for no mayonnaise on their sandwich, not to finish the entire meal, or not to go to fast food restaurants at all. Some people argue that companies do not force people to eat their food. Some believe that buying groceries and cooking at home instead can be cheaper and healthier. Cooking at home and enjoying a meal with the family is also more appealing than eating quickly at a fast food restaurant. Eating at home is also advantageous because one can control the portions. Although this could be helpful, many do not have the time to go to the grocery store and then cook a meal after working all day.

Consumers are not only responsible for what they eat, but also for exercising off their fat and calorie intake. The consumer has the responsibility to exercise regularly. As Barry Glassner, author of "Environmental Factors and Genetics Are the Source of Obesity" simply states, "Over-weight results from one thing: eating more food than one burns in physical activity." Many advertisements tell us how to improve our body shape by buying exercise equipment or going to the gym. Unfortunately, many people simply do not make time. If people are going to eat fast food, they should be more disciplined about exercising. However, with the high calories and fat content in these meals, to burn off all those calories is harder with the little time busy individuals have to exercise.

Adding a "so-what" factor to the argument, clarifying its importance

Many children and adults in this country are facing a serious problem. Obesity has led to many deaths, including heart disease, diabetes, and many other serious medical conditions. Fast food is not the only cause of obesity, but it is also a substantial promoter. It is true that fast food franchises do not force anybody to buy their food. However, the advertising and cheap prices are misleading and enticing. The unhealthy fat content in these products is extremely high. Yet, these companies promote "bigger as better" in their advertisements. With many people having busy schedules, fast food is the easiest solution. However, fast food franchises should be liable for obesity in the United States, because they know how much fat they have in their products, which is extremely unhealthy, but they still encourage people to buy their food.

WORKS CITED

Balko, Radley. "Obesity Is Not a Public Health Issue." *Current Controversies: Food.* Ed. Jan Grover. Detroit: Greenhaven Press, 2008. *Opposing Viewpoints Resource Center.* Gale. Web. 20 Oct 2009.

Buchholz, Todd G. "Fast Food Should Not Be Blamed for Obesity." *Opposing Viewpoints: Food.* Ed. Laura K. Egendorf. Detroit: Greenhaven Press, 2006. *Opposing Viewpoints Resource Center.* Gale. Web. 9 Oct. 2009

Engler, Yves. "Much of the Responsibility for Obesity Lies with Corporations."*Opposing Viewpoints: Obesity.* Ed. Andrea C. Nakaya. San Diego: Greenhaven Press, 2006. *Opposing Viewpoints Resource Center.* Gale. Web. 7 Oct. 2009.

Glassner, Barry. "Environmental Factors and Genetics Are the Source of Obesity." *Current Controversies: Food.* Ed. Jan Grover. Detroit: Greenhaven Press, 2008. *Opposing Viewpoints Resource Center.* Gale. Web. 18 Oct. 2009.

Nestle, Marion. "The Fast Food Industry Intentionally Markets Unhealthy Foods to Children." *At Issue: Fast Food.* Ed. Tracy Brown Collins. San Diego: Greenhaven Press, 2005. *Opposing Viewpoints Resource Center.* Gale. Web. 11 Oct. 2009.

Simon, Michele. "Even the 'Healthy' Choices at Fast-Food Restaurants Are Unhealthy." *At Issue: Fast Food.* Ed. Roman Espejo. Detroit: Greenhaven Press, 2009. *Opposing Viewpoints Resource Center.* Gale. Web. 10 Oct. 2009.

Stern, Seth. "Fast Food Is Linked to Obesity and Other Serious Health Problems." *At Issue: Fast Food.* Ed. Roman Espejo. Detroit: Greenhaven Press, 2009. *Opposing Viewpoints Resource Center.* Gale. Web. 19 Oct. 2009.

In alphabetical order, following MLA format rules

ANNOTATED BIBLIOGRAPHY

Adrianna Saavedra

Stern, Seth. "Fast Food Is Linked to Obesity and Other Serious Health Problems." *At Issue: Fast Food.* Ed. Roman Espejo. Detroit: Greenhaven Press, 2009. *Opposing Viewpoints Resource Center.* Gale. 7 Oct. 2009.

Seth Stern argues that fast food is linked to obesity in many ways. Through advertising, fast food franchises reach many people, especially children, persuading them to eat their food. Stern points out how many people are surprised to see that their calorie intake for one day could be used up in just one meal. These companies are misleading in their advertising, causing some to overeat and become obese.

Yves Engler. "Much of the Responsibility for Obesity Lies with Corporations." *Opposing Viewpoints: Obesity.* Ed. Andrea C. Nakaya. San Diego: Greenhaven Press, 2006. *Opposing Viewpoints Resource Center.* Gale. 7 Oct. 2009.

Yves Engler explains the significant problem that obesity is becoming in the U. S. Engler accounts for many other diseases such as heart disease, diabetes, and cancers that are caused because of obesity. Many people are buying more fast food, which is often more convenient than cooking at home. Engler describes how fast food companies target children because they influence their parents. This causes people to overeat unhealthy products because of the persuasion that the companies' food is better and more delicious. Engler also states that the reason why people go to fast food franchises is that they struggle at work and get tired, which leads to exercising less and eating more.

CRITICAL THINKING AND RESPONSE QUESTIONS

1. Reflect upon the strategies the writers used in their cover letters. Is one approach more effective than the other? Use this information to create your own cover letter.

2. Identify instances of ethos, pathos, and logos in Lauren Manke's essay "Stem Cells: From Rats to Humans." Locate an example in the essay that successfully uses Aristotle's Argumentative Appeals and explain why it is effective.

3. In his essay "Cold, Hungry, and Homeless: A Second Chance for the Forgotten People," Arthur Azatyan uses a personal anecdote to support his argument that not all homeless people reflect the public stereotype of homelessness. Does his use of a personal anecdote make his essay more effective? Is the anecdote appropriate to the discussion? Why or why not? As a type of proof, would you classify Azatyan's anecdote as an example of ethos, pathos, or logos?

4. In the essay "Make the Rhythms Heard in Public Education," can you identify a clear thesis? Is this thesis evident in the body paragraphs? You may choose to make an outline to map the development.

5. Examine an essay of your choosing. Make a note of how it is organized. Where does the thesis statement appear? How are the body paragraphs structured? At what point does a counterargument appear? Does this arrangement strengthen or weaken the author's overall purpose?

6. Pick an essay that effectively uses transitional phrases, or effectively transitions from one argument to the next, and discuss how the transitions contribute to the coherence of the essay as a whole.

7. Some of these essays address an article that the reader may not have read. Reflect upon an essay in which you have not read the primary source. How does this writer familiarize the subject matter?

8. Review the works cited information for some of the essays. Make a list of sources that you believe are credible and a list of sources that you do not think are very credible. In a short paragraph or two, explain what makes sources credible

9. Pick any essay from *Wings* and refute it in an essay of your own, or expand upon the given essay, adding and strengthening the original argument.

10. Garrick Raigosa titles his essay about the debate on the negative effects of video games, "Do You Feel Violent after Playing Pong?" Is the title relevant to the essay? Does it give the reader some clue of what to expect in the essay? Why or why not?

IN-CLASS ESSAY
Marlene Lopez

Using the article and other outside sources, explain your position on society's addiction to technology OR the internet.

Instructor: Michele Mayle

In order to get my papers to sound good I have to review them several times, which is the reason why I find in-class essays to be so complicated. However, I found this in-class essay a lot easier to write. When I started writing this essay, I tried to come up with three main points that I wanted to discuss and then I went on from there. I think once you brainstorm your ideas, it becomes a lot easier to write an entire essay in a short amount of time.

The article "Net Addiction Declared Disorder" by Ruth Hill states that some countries like China believe that internet addiction is a disorder. However, other people believe that those who are addicted to the internet do not necessarily suffer from a disorder; they would rather think of it as 'pathological internet use.' The people who do not believe internet addiction is a disorder argue that pathological internet use is a better term because these are people that have other disorders and use the internet as a way of coping with or expressing other problems. The article states that some people, like NetSafe spokesman John Fenaughty, ask the question whether it is fair to label internet addiction the same way we would label an addiction having to do with drugs. Although some people believe being addicted to the internet is considered a disorder, it is not because in some cases it is only an apparent symptom to other problems; it is something that does not cause us any health related issues, and it can only be another ordinary addiction.

Internet addiction can be a simple way of coping with or expressing other disorders. There are times when kids spend hours on the internet instead of doing homework, but this does not necessarily mean the child suffers from an "internet addiction disorder." It could be that the child is only using the internet as a way of escaping from his or her school related problems, or maybe the child suffers from ADD and uses the internet as a way of entertainment. The case might also be where a person suffers from some sort of anxiety and uses the internet for relaxation or coping. People that might be considered addicted to the internet have other underlying issues and use the internet to express their problems.

The article mentions whether it is fair to label an internet addiction the same way we would label a drug addiction, and the answer is no. It makes absolutely no sense to think of this as a disorder when in fact it causes no harm to others or to the person addicted. Being addicted to a technological device is not the same as being addicted to alcohol or drugs. Constantly browsing the web or spending many hours on the internet does not cause any health related problems. As long as a person does not let the internet interfere with his or her life, there is no reason why the internet should be considered harmful. I find that I can spend numerous hours online and I do not suffer from an internet disorder. I do consider myself being addicted to the internet; however, it is not something that is causing me harm. My constant need to use the internet is due to the way our society works. We all rely on the internet, whether it is for work, school, or to communicate; it is something that we all use. The only difference is that some like it more than others.

Internet addiction can be the same as any other addiction. Some people are addicted to certain foods, others to a certain lip-gloss, a specific flavor of gum, or a certain game and it does not mean that it is a disorder. People are usually bound to get attached to something and it does not mean they should be treated for it. Teenagers especially are always finding new things that they become completely reliant upon, to the point where they feel they need it to survive. This generation revolves around technology; it is the way people today communicate. It should not be considered a disorder, but it should be treated as a harmless addiction.

There are some people who think of internet addiction as a disorder. The article mentions that in some cases people are treated for it. They believe that if people spend many hours on the internet or feel anxious when the server crashes, they are suffering from a disorder that needs some sort of cure. However, a cure should be used when the addiction is causing harmful results, and using the internet is only a way of expressing other disorders that do not need a cure. People are as addicted to the internet as they are to their cell phones, but it is something we all need. Maybe in the future a new invention will come out and people will be addicted to this new invention too. After a while, things tend to get boring. Someone who was once addicted to a game after playing it for so long will decide to move on to something new. It is the same thing when we talk about the internet; right now is the time when everyone is "crazy" about the internet, but once something new comes out, they will forget all about it.

People that are addicted to the internet are still able to live a normal life and it has no effect on the way one behaves. If it does, then it probably means that the internet addiction is not so much the problem, but there is something else. There is nothing wrong with liking something too much. At one point, we all feel the need to use or have something. Therefore, internet addiction is not a disorder.

FIRST IMPRESSIONS: COVER LETTERS

"Be aware of your sources. Use credible sources,
not sources like Google. You already know
Trent is as unreliable as Wikipedia."

—ERIC SAENZ

A CONVERSATION DURING COMBAT
Eric Saenz

Instructor: Sevan Salibian

What inspired me to write this cover letter is the fact that coming to college, I absolutely hated writing until I took English 155. Though I do not love writing essays, I do not go through as much stress as I used to when assigned to write an essay. I wrote this dialogue script to express my thoughts after taking English 155. This script shows my improvements in writing effective essays.

Alex: Eric! Shoot the man on your left, he has us cornered!

Eric: I don't see him.

Alex: Oh man, I'll take him. Instead of taking English 155, you should have trained more on your shooting range and accuracy. How are we supposed to win this war if you can't shoot in open sea?

Eric: Hey man, don't say that. English 155 taught me many things I could use during war, maybe even more than shooting training would have.

Alex: Yeah right kid, you're too slow. I'm scared for you.

Eric: Don't be, I am more prepared than you could ever be.

Alex: Ha, ha, ha. How?

Eric: Remember when you ran inside the fallen airplane? You were lucky I was there and was able to shoot the enemy before they killed you.

Alex: So what? What does that have to do with English 155?

Eric: English 155 taught me that before I respond to an assignment, I should brainstorm by using methods like free-writing and bubbles to come up with an outline or plan. It helps me be more organized. If I had been in your position, I would've come up with a plan before running inside the plane; I wouldn't have been shot at. Also, pay attention to the smaller things like grammar and mechanics. I have definitely improved. Before English 155, I didn't even know what a run-on or fragment was. More practice would be helpful though.

Alex: Yeah, well Trent told me the airplane was clear.

Eric: Be aware of your sources. Use credible sources, not sources like Google. You already know Trent is as unreliable as Wikipedia.

Alex: Well, who cares what you say, at least my language is formal.

Eric: You don't need your language to be entirely formal. When you talk to me, it is completely informal. My writing language is not supposed to be entirely formal. I can use my voice as well.

Alex: Dude, you're making me mad. Stop criticizing me!

Eric: Well, peer review is helpful, man. It can help improve what you are doing or writing. All those peer reviews during SI were extremely helpful. They helped me construct more ideas for my essays.

Alex: Whatever, dude.

Eric: Before you say something like 'English 155 is a waste of time,' come up with a good argument or thesis to back it up. Though, I do agree with your point that I should have practiced my shooting accuracy and range.

Alex: Don't take my side now, Eric. It's too late.

Eric: I am only considering the counterargument, like one should always do in an argumentative essay.

Alex: Dude, I got to go. We'll continue playing *Modern Warfare 2* later.

Eric: Yeah, me too; I have to choose two of my essays and revise them for my portfolio. Should be fun now that I know how to write an effective essay. Talk to you later.

A HISTORY OF A WRITER'S PROGRESS
Elisabeth Brock

Instructor: Beverly Cope

Finally, I felt free to express myself as I liked. I was given leave to choose any style to write my reflective introduction for my portfolio, and I eagerly took advantage of the opportunity. But, at first, with so many possible avenues of expression before me, I was hesitant concerning what style to adopt. Eventually, after much thought and deliberation, I resolved to model my paper after Shakespeare's Romeo and Juliet, *one of my absolute favorites. Writing this paper was the most enjoyable writing experience that I have had all semester, and I am very grateful to have had this opportunity to express myself without being shackled by any restrictions or requirements.*

THE ACTORS

ELISABETH, a young and blossoming writer; freshman at California State University of Northridge

AN ENGLISH PROFESSOR, teacher to Elisabeth

THE CHORUS

SCENE: California State University, Northridge

THE PROLOGUE
Enter Chorus.

CHORUS:

Two writers both alike in proficiency
(in fair Northridge, where we lay our scene)
From beginning to struggle, arrived at competency,
Professor professed, her pupil to refine,
And student studied, gath'ring wisdom, benign.
For 'twas Teacher's task her pupil to instruct,
Her faults to mend, her strengths deduct.
And behold, o'er the course, semester long,
Pupil transformed, from weak to strong.
And now remains but to persuade
The audience who now shall pick the grade.
For theirs is leave to choose her fate:
Be she writer poor or writer great?
The proof of this developed, young sage
Is the two scenes traffic of our page,
To which if you with gentle eyes await
What here shall miss, our toil shall articulate.
Exeunt.

ACT FIRST

SCENE first. Northridge. A classroom on the campus. Elisabeth is sitting at her desk. Enter Professor.

PROFESSOR: God ye good morrow, Elisabeth. Anon? Be you so eager to begin that you do arrive in my chamber before the appointed hour has struck? Or perchance I was unclear in my specification?

ELISABETH: Nay, good lady, thou did'st verify it well. My reason for my earliness is accounted to my resolve to be sure to avoid lateness.

PROFESSOR: Merry well, my good pupil, thy fortitude is commendable…

Bell tolls the fourth hour of the afternoon.

And now that the hour is upon us, let the instruction commence. I would begin by offering critique of your first paper.

ELISABETH: I would fain receive all the correction that you would supply, Madam Professor.

PROFESSOR: Overall, I dub it a "good paper!" Your introduction is "nice." But format and spacing is cause for some vice. Dropped words here and there create mild confusion. DO NOT hide your thesis in blended delusion. Your wording is sometimes unclear or redundant. I approve of your backing with sources abundant, but cite them correctly as MLA specifies. Never use 'you's,' I'll allow use of 'I's.'

ELISABETH: I recognize my faults that you have pointed out. Now to re-till and re-plant, that new strengths may yet sprout.

Exeunt.

SCENE second. Same venue. Clock strikes the fourth hour. Enter Professor.

PROFESSOR: God ye good morrow, Elisabeth. What of the improvements that I proposed when we were last in company yester week? Did you make use of the knowledge that I bestowed upon you, my fine scholar?

ELISABETH: By my troth, I believe I have, good teacher, and I trust your delight at the revision. Here in this, my second essay, I incorporated all your past advice and with it forged a double-edged argument. I am fairly confident that this second essay meets the bar.

Hands over second essay. Professor reads thoroughly.

PROFESSOR: Indeed, I find little to critique in this, your second trial. Your thesis is strongly situated, your formatting is accurate, your articulation precise, and your sentences flow in seamless unity. But still here I see grammatical errors sprinkled throughout, and your in-text citations require slight alterations. All-comprehending, this essay surpasses your last. I set for you a standard, and over it you passed. As for your final essay, make it sublime, for 'twill be graded by eyes other than mine. Demonstrate the qualities you've shown to me and affirm that you are what you ought to be. Elaborate on the knowledge you've gained of English. The rubric requirements are yours to distinguish.

ELISABETH: O Rubric, Rubric, wherefore art thou so ambiguous? Yet despite your nebulous nature, I have still grasped hold of your meaning. You require that I correctly articulate and formulate each of my ideas into properly constructed sentences, unhindered by grammatical errors. You have specified that my organization should be clear and logical, following spatial, chronological, or progressive strategies. You desire a strong thesis that's supported by a firm foundation of qualified evidence. Can I ever meet your high standards? I believe I can.

But it is not by my spoken word that this I can attest, but by my written work which tells it best.

For never is a writer's progress better shown than through witnessing her birth and how she's grown.

Exeunt.

AMERICAN POLITICS

"Now is not the time to look away with fear as another hurricane claims more lives or turn the other cheek with apathy as the welfare of another species is placed in perilous jeopardy."

—SIDNEY JONES

THE GREATEST: ONE BANK TO RULE THEM ALL

Sean Smith

Instructor: Terri Silverberg

Pick a problem. How can this problem be alleviated or resolved?

During the semester, we have discussed several controversies from varying points of view. This assignment requires choosing a specific social, economic, political, civic or environmental issue that you care about and wish to see resolved.

There are few creations of the federal government that are as misunderstood as the Federal Reserve System, sometimes referred to as the Fed or Federal Reserve. Often called the fourth branch of the United States Government, the Fed has many fervent critics who are convinced that it can do no good because of its design as a central bank. These critics believe that the Fed devalues the American Dollar (USD) and is controlled by Wall Street investors who have no interest in improving the lives of middle-class families. Ron Paul, a Congressional Representative from Texas and longtime member of the House's Committee on Financial Service, even goes as far as saying, "there is no authority in the constitution...There should be no Fed" (Paul). These are questionably valid claims, but these individuals fail to see the vital role that the Federal Reserve plays in our economy. As with all aspects of government, the Fed has its own problems to overcome. That is, however, no reason to advocate its destruction. The Federal Reserve should remain in place because it provides stability to the economy, enables effective monetary policy, and is a regulator independent of the Federal government.

The Federal Reserve provides much needed stability to the economy that cannot be easily generated elsewhere. There are many regulators in the economy such as the Securities Exchange Commission, but few have the power and scope of the Fed. David Wessel, a Pulitzer Prize winner and Wall Street Journal writer, states that the Fed has the ability to adjust what is called the "discount rate," the interest rate that banks use when charging other banks for loans (Wessel 99). Inflation, one of the most debilitating economic events, is countered through the use of the discount rate. When inflation begins to appear, the Federal Reserve raises the discount rate and decreases the amount of effective currency in circulation (Greenspan 154). This action also has the effect of slowed growth because banks will only lend at a higher rate so it is more difficult to take out a loan.

Opponents of the Federal Reserve often cite the discount rate as their first point of contention. During the 1990s, the discount rate was held at historically low levels and this, in turn, caused another effect of a low discount rate, asset bubbles or investments that are speculatively made over a short period of time. An asset bubble occurs when loans are incredibly easy to acquire, so they begin to be given to individuals or markets that cannot support their own growth. This has been seen most recently in the 2009 housing asset bubble. Critics say that the discount rate directly contributed to the housing bubble and that without artificially low rates an asset bubble would have never occurred. Ron Paul, as previously mentioned, is one of the Fed's most adamant critics in Congress. He believes that the Fed "purposely lowers interest rates with no regard to effects of inflation" (Paul).

This can be seen most recently in the Fed reaction to the housing crisis. Paul believes that the Fed is injecting ludicrous amounts of money into the economy and consequently is inflating the USD.

These critics are correct in saying that the Federal Reserve held rates too low for too long. The discount rate does, however, provide a valuable tool for stabilizing the economy in times of inflation or deflation. This ability should not be revoked because it was irresponsibly used in the 1990s. The positive power of the discount rate became apparent when the 2007 recession began to occur when the Federal Reserve realized that a powerful recession was about to occur the used in the 1990s. The positive power of the discount rate became apparent when the 2007 recession began to occur. When the Federal Reserve realized that a powerful recession was about to occur, it quickly began to lower the discount rate. This increased the liquidity or ability for money to shift between different industries of the economies. Most economists believe that an illiquid economy during a recession has a high probability to turn into a depression (Wessel 35). As to Ron Paul, the Fed has been injecting large amounts of money into the markets but not without reason. According to the United States Department of Labor, the agency responsible for calculating inflation, the United States is experiencing a period of deflation. The Fed had watched deflation cause a major recession in Asia and was determined to fight in America (Wessel 78). The discount rate proved to be the perfect tool to fight deflation of the USD in the current financial crisis. If the Fed had not lowered rates, as Paul would advocate, the economy would have been starved of dollars and damaged unnecessarily. The Federal Reserve is the only entity that has the ability to effectively combat a forming recession before it fully develops.

The Federal Reserve has many unique powers that allow it to administer monetary policy. Regulators, such as the Securities Exchange Commission, also play an important role in regulating the economy. They ensure that companies provide accurate information about their financial actions so individuals can confidently invest. These regulators, however, pose no occurrence that, when recessions hit, individuals transfer their investments to the USD (Wessel 140). They do this because the USD is a stable currency that is a better alternative to higher risk investments like derivative. This created a precarious situation at the beginning of the current recession for foreign central banks; they were running out of dollars. The Federal Reserve saw this situation developing and extended loans to these banks in order to relieve that pressure on the USD. These loans were staggering in size and totaled over half a trillion dollar (*State of the Economy*). Many critics saw the size of these loans on the Federal Reserve's balance sheet and took it as a prime opportunity to attack the central bank. For example, representative Alan Grayson aggressively questioned chairman Bernanke about the Fed lending money to foreign central (*State of the Economy*). Grayson is of the belief that by lending to foreign governments, the Fed is forgetting the people it is designed to protect. This criticism is entirely unfounded because it lacks an understanding of what the Fed's role is. The Federal Reserve was not designed to only lend American banks; it was meant to provide stability to an entire economy. The Federal Reserve, as quoted form the Federal Reserve Act of 1913, is tasked with "maintain[ing] long run growth of the monetary and credit[ing] aggregates commensurate with the economy's long run potential to increase production, so as to promote effectively the goals of maximum employment and stable prices" (H.R. 7837). The destabilization of the dollar abroad would have a resounding affect on our economy because the USD would become higher in demand and there would be less to meet this demand. This scenario is called deflation and is equally as debilitating as inflation and has caused recessions on its own. Christopher Conte, a writer for *CQ Researcher*, states that Asia, in particular, suffered a severe recession in the 1990s caused by deflation (Conte 1). This set of scenarios would allow the Fed to combat stable prices. The Federal Reserve is a prime example of a central bank wielding effective monetary policy.

The Federal Reserve is crucial to the economy because it has an unprecedented level of independence from the Federal government. When the Federal Reserve System was created in 1913, it was seen as possibly dangerous because it would have almost no accountability in Congress and would wield the power to either cripple or enhance the United States economy (H.R. 7837). It was also considered dangerous because many of its members are bankers, not politicians or voters. To add a check, Congress included a provision in the Federal Open Market Committee (FOMC). This committee is composed of five regional bank presidents and the seven governors selected by the President of the United States. This composition gives the Fed as much political independence as possible. The governors are frequently replaced and have little reason to make their decisions politically because they have come from large banks before serving as governors. The Fed Chairman is the one position that is subject to intense political pressure because he or she must face reappointment every four years. Alan Greenspan, a former chairman of the Fed, reports that "When I told George H. W. Bush that we were going to raise rates, he looked at me and jabbed his fist into his stomach and said 'You're hitting me right here!'" (111). President Bush Sr. then went on about how the Fed was "not being responsible to the real needs of the country" (111). The position of chairman has, however, remained relatively apolitical as of late because presidents have a tendency to approve a prior president's chairman, regardless of political affiliations (146). All-in-all, this makes the Federal Reserve a relatively apolitical entity. This is fortunate because, through history, central banks with higher levels of political independence also have better success at combating inflation. Central banks that are political tend to be pushed around by the governing bodies, which have little idea how to manage a complex economy.

The Federal Reserve often gets a negative reputation from politicians. Many have a disdain for the Federal Reserve because of its political independence and unaccountability. These complaints are, however, largely based on a fear of what the Fed might do, not what it has done. The Federal Reserve has proven that it is an indispensable central bank that plays a vital role in all aspects of the economy. It failed in the fact that it kept interest rates too low for too long, but this does not diminish the tremendous amount of good it does. It is capable of exacting effective monetary policy with relatively few political pressures. The Federal Reserve System is an efficient central bank that provides confidence and stability to the economy.

Works Cited

Conte, Christopher. "Deflation Fears: Are Falling Princes a Bigger Threat than Inflation?" *CQ Researcher* (Feb 1998). Web. 18 Nov. 2009.

Greenspan, Alan. *The Age of Turbulence.* New York: Penguin Group, 2007. Print.

H.R. 7837, 36rd Cong., United States Statues at Large (1913) (enacted). Print.

Paul, Ron. "Ron Paul's Campaign for Liberty." Rally for the Republic. Minneapolis. 18 Nov. 2009. Speech.

Ron Paul: The Entire Economic System is Subprime, 110th Cong. (2008) (testimony of Ron Paul). Print.

State of the Economy & Monetary Policy, 111th Cong. (2009) (testimony of Alan Grayson). Print.

Wessel, David. *In Fed We trust.* New York: Crown Business, 2009. Print.

STEM CELLS: FROM RATS TO HUMANS

Lauren Manke

Instructor: Ashlyn Morse

Imagine that you are writing a proposal to Congress. In this proposal, you will either choose to convince Congress to increase federal funding for embryonic stem cell research, or you will convince Congress that you want embryonic stem cell research further regulated.

It is safe to say that we have all experienced someone close to us die, suffer from disease, or rely on organ transplants as a way of survival. My grandmother suffers from Lymphoma for the fourth time, kidney failure and liver failure and the chance for survival is slim. Those in need rely on medical abilities, but even the current advancements prove to be useless. Embryonic stem cell research is what many scientists have found to be the answer, giving us the opportunity to cure diseases, heal and repair damaged body parts and have a greater understanding of the human body. After all, shouldn't saving and preserving the human body be at the top of the government's list?

Several rats stare death in the face as the nerve disease they carry threatens their individual existence. Their future is now in the hands of several scientists from Johns Hopkins Medical Institution. These 15 rats are injected with embryonic stem cells in the hopes of reviving their virus-damaged spinal cords. On June 26, 2006, to the surprise of many, eleven of the fifteen rats injected with embryonic stem cells gained partial recovery from their paralysis and were able to put weight on their previously paralyzed limbs ("Scientists"). Imagine what the outcomes of this procedure could have on humans who suffer from paralysis and nerve damage. Imagine the lives that can be restored and the opportunities that can be made for those who are currently limited by disease. Although there is a strong opposing force against embryonic stem cell research, embryonic stem cell research should receive an increase in federal funding because the breakthrough of stem cell research has offered opportunities to cure diseases, heal damaged body parts, and provide greater understanding of the human body. Embryonic stem cell research has become one of the biggest controversies that American politics faces and it continues to prove to be a necessary advancement in this scientific world, yet it is in dire need of federal funding.

Diseases have threatened many lives and the idea of being cured through stem cells has given hope to many. The advancement of science has given scientists that ability to further continue their discoveries and, if researchers can alter stem cells into regular cells, then these cells could be put back into the body to replace those cells that are defective. The newly converted cells could give physicians the chance to cure many maladies, such as Parkinson's and leukemia, because the failing cells would be taken out and replaced with the stem cells which would help fight off the particular disease (Easterbrook 5). Just like the rats injected with embryonic stem cells at Johns Hopkins Medical Institution, humans will have a chance to be helped or cured of their own diseases and other "maladies." Although this is seen as currently theoretical, the idea of stem cells saving lives has been highly looked upon by many scientists and doctors.

Because stem cells are not only limited in helping diseases, those in need of organ transplants or suffering from damaged body parts can also be saved through stem cells. Embryonic stem cells have the capability of "metamorphosing into any component of the body: heart, nerves, blood, bone, and muscle" (Easterbrook 2). This means that these stem cells can be used to recreate specific organs or other body components to replace those that have been damaged. A study in 1997 revealed that "about 56,000 people in the United States alone were awaiting organ transplants" and "about 4,000 died while waiting" (Wertz 12). With the advancements in science and the potential benefits that stem cells can provide, Gregg Easterbrook noted that "the need for donor organs for heart or liver transplants might fade, as new body parts are cultured artificially" (Easterbrook 5). As clearly seen by the study in 1997, organ donors are dramatically more rare than the patients in need of the organs themselves. This continues to prove the strong need for the development of embryonic stem cells in the hopes that many of these patients can be saved.

Embryonic stem cells not only provide millions of patients with a greater probability of enjoying life, but they also allow scientists to further their understanding of the human body and the millions of cells that comprise it. Because embryonic stem cells are "capable of becoming or 'differentiating' into virtually any cell type" ("New Limits" 3), what limits scientists from studying the embryonic cells themselves? The answer is simply nothing. Cells are the functional units of multicellular organisms. That is, they make up every living thing. It is because of this that scientists can use the research of stem cells to "study the cytology of conception" (Easterbrook 1). After all, reproduction is one of the prime characteristics of life. With this understanding of the basic units of life, cells, scientists will have the capability of understanding why our life form is prone to certain diseases and possibly be able to find ways to prevent these diseases (Easterbrook 5). However, because possible outcomes of stem cell research are not perfected, not guaranteed, and some take issue with its morality, some people are against this research.

Some of the biggest concerns of stem cell research are summed up in a journal entry: "New limits of funding stem cell research questioned." Specific concerns that stem cell supporters face include ethical standards, stem cells having sufficient genetic diversity, the safety of its use in humans, and whether the stem cells could be received quickly and for minimal cost ("New Limits" 8). Although all of these are viable concerns to this research, several of them stand out more than others: ethical standards and cost. What should first be clarified is where embryonic stem cells come from. The key way the researchers harvest these stem cells are through in vitro fertility clinics, or IVF clinics. Here, the extra fertilized eggs that are not used are saved. It is from these blastocysts, five day old fertilized eggs, that embryonic stem cells are taken from and used for research. With the concerns for ethicality comes one of the biggest questions and debates: are early embryos human beings? This question leads us to yet another question: what defines a human being? Andrew Sullivan states that "stem cell research enthusiasts say we are defined by our DNA" and "the embryo contains exactly the same amount of genetic information as you or I do. We aren't different from it in kind, only different in degree: in age, size, weight, gender and on and on" (Sullivan 7).

If these embryos are, in fact, to be considered human beings, then they must "deserve all the rights of human beings, especially the right to respect and dignity" (Sullivan 1), as all human beings deserve. Sullivan's comments assume the religious viewpoint that "embryos have immortal souls, and that is why they are worthy of greater protection than nonhuman animals" (Singer 6). But if this is so, then what has happened to the separation of religion and state? Is it not stated in the United States constitution that government and religious institutions are to be separated from each other? If religion and state are not separated, then, as stated by Peter Singer, "nonreligious citizens of the United States continue to be disadvantaged by the strength of religious belief in this country" (Singer 6). But what establishes that these embryos are alive and that religion and morality are to be a deciding factor in stem cell research? Again, we must look at what defines a life.

Although many agree with Sullivan's statement that embryos are indeed humans, others believe differently. Early human embryos that are used in harvesting stem cells lack important characteristics of humans and, therefore, "there is no reason to object to research conducted on a being that has no brain, consciousness, preferences of any kind, or capacity of suffering" (Singer 1). Therefore, the ethical issues based on the idea that the embryos used in stem cell research are living beings cannot control the decisions of the progress of this research because there is no exact scientific (or policy) agreement that human embryos at an early stage are considered living beings. The embryos used in stem cell research are already on the path of death in that they will be discarded thus ending their chance at life to begin with, assuming that the argument that these embryos are human beings and alive is viable. Considering this, Gregg Easterbrook brings up another question: "do we ban research on the aborted out of a sense of guilt that we should not add mutilation to the wrongs suffered by a life denied" (Easterbrook 16)? Having no brain, consciousness and other necessities needed in life, there can be no concrete reasoning that these embryos are in fact alive without any evidence.

The concern of federal funding for embryonic stem cell research has become a huge issue in the progress of stem cell based discoveries. Stem cell research could potentially take many years to perfect, which would require a continual amount of money to be available to researchers in order to continue to conduct this research. Stem cell research is also only in its beginning stage which means that "private industries are reluctant to invest in such an early-stage research [causing] progress toward medical therapies likely to be hindered without government funding" ("New Limits" 4). Although the concerns for stem cell research are understandable, what isn't understandable is the reason why the government is not acting on the chance to save and protect the human race. Having the opportunity to cure diseases, repair and grow damaged body parts, and have a better understanding of the human body and life itself are significant medical advancements that can foreshadow what the future holds for the scientific world: further scientific breakthroughs and the potential to save thousands of lives. As shown in the 1997 study, thousands of people await organs and, in a bigger sense, await the chance at life itself. To deny the opportunity to study stem cells is essentially denying life. After all, stem cells, as described by Peter singer, "hold limitless promise for medical research" (Singer 1), and this medical research are what many depend on.

Works Cited

Easterbrook, Gregg. "Cloning and a change in the meaning of life: stem-cell research." *Current*. 413 (June 1999): 19(7). *Opposing Viewpoints Resource Center*. Gale. Web. 25 Sep. 2009

"New limits on funding of stem cell research questioned." *Issues in Science and Technology*. 18. 1 (Fall 2001): 29. *Opposing Viewpoints Resource Center*. Gale. Web. 25 Sep. 2009

"Scientists use embryonic stem cells to awaken latent motor nerve repair." *The Medical News*. News—Medical.net, 26 June, 2006. Web. 25 Sep. 2009.

Singer, Peter. "Research Using Human Embryos Is Morally Acceptable." *At Issue: The Ethics of Abortion*. Ed. Jennifer A. Hurley. San Diego: Greenhaven Press, 2001. *Opposing Viewpoints Resource Center*. Gale. Web. 25 Sep. 2009

Sullivan, Andrew. "Early Human Embryos Are Human Beings." *At Issue: Human Embryo Experimentation*. Ed. Roman Espejo. San Diego: Greenhaven Press, 2002. *Opposing Viewpoints Resource Center*. Gale. Web. 25 Sep. 2009

Wertz, Dorothy C. "Fetal Tissue Research Will Benefit Medical Science." *Current Controversies: The Abortion Controversy*. Ed. Lynette Knapp. San Diego: Greenhaven Press, 2001. *Opposing Viewpoints Resource Center*. Gale. Web. 25 Sep. 2009

GLOBAL WARMING: A PERILOUS CHALLENGE FOR THE NEW MILLENNIUM

Sidney Jones

Instructor: Terri Silverberg

Pick a problem. Discuss how it can be alleviated or resolved.

When I found out that the final task in the gauntlet of Honors English 155 was an essay that involved identifying a relevant problem and crafting an effective solution, doubt and anxiety immediately began to infiltrate my mind. While I have always been a passionate advocate for environmental reform, the monotonous nature of traditional schooling (while unintentional) embedded within me a belief in the importance of being a productive yet passive member of society. In retrospect, when I reflect on this assignment, the most important lesson I learned was not necessarily how to write an exemplary persuasive essay, but how to take the tools we learn in school and apply them to the issues we face. In parallel to global warming, education can also wreak destruction if it is ignored and forced to foster reactive unconsciousness rather than proactive action.

Sheets of glacial ice melting into the still waters, violent hurricanes obliterating cities, excruciating heat waves leaving villages barren—these environmental realities represent the current issue of global warming. This ecological crisis is due to the gradual increase in the Earth's temperature caused by the release of greenhouse gases like carbon dioxide and methane into the Earth's atmosphere. These gases act as a blanket around the Earth, trapping larger amounts of solar heat than the atmosphere would normally retain. With a noticeable increase in natural disasters, a concern about global warming is on the minds of many across the world, but how can we curtail this ongoing disaster? The federal government should install a cap-and-trade policy on companies and factories in order to help combat the gradual increase of sea levels, improve air quality, and create eco-friendly jobs.

Many people perceive global warming as a mythical giant, fostered by melodramatic assumptions. One example is former Vice President Al Gore's prediction that in "ten years" the ice body of Greenland will "break up and slip into the sea," which Patrick Michaels, a senior fellow at the Cato Institute, a public policy research facility, and Robert Balling Jr. a professor of geography at Arizona State University, note is an overstatement that is "unchallenged" by the science community (1). Whether we reflect on the immense anxiety before the ill-fated year of Y2K, or the Christian Evangelicals' false prophecy of the Earth's demise in the 1980s, every generation has believed they were going to be the last. As the first decade of the new millennium comes to an end, this anxiety for the unknown future surfaces once again. As a result, natural occurrences like glacial melting are seen as the metaphorical monster many feel will devour humanity. More importantly, Michaels and Balling refer to global warming as a political strategy used to gain support because "elected officials" don't want to be "ostracized" by holding "unpopular views" against global warming (5). This is a valid point, as history shows that the federal government often takes action whether right or wrong to abate public tension. Consider the signing of

Executive Order 9066, which strived to curb the overwhelming fear of a Japanese insurgency in the United States, by interning Americans of Japanese descent in camps, or the Palmer raids, which functioned to alleviate people's worries about a national communist revolt by staging unwarranted searches of suspected socialists' homes and offices.

The government's decision to hold back the wave of alarm towards global warming, along with Obama's recent passing of an $825 billion stimulus package that allotted money for renewable energy research, do not negate the fact that the current climate crisis is an issue. Greenland may not drift off into sea in a handful of years, but Colin Woodard, journalist for *The Christian Science Monitor,* acknowledges that the body of ice in this land has diminished by "6 percent since 1978" and its thickness has declined by "40 percent in recent decades" (29). These statistics reveal a subtle omen that if no significant measures are taken to improve the environment's health, it will decompose over time. This disintegration may be a gradual process, but destruction is nonetheless taking place. More illustrations of the Earth's obliteration include freelance journalist Stephan Faris' observation of the "fourteen hurricanes" unleashed in 2005 with four at "category five status" (38), animals like the polar bear becoming endangered species (153), and the crushing heat waves that took place in Europe in 2003 (133) killing thousands of people. While the earth is a variable entity ridden with tumultuous storms and variations in temperature, the rapidity of these drastic changes in weather, in animal populations, and the environments they reside in sheds light on the presence of an outside force—which is global warming.

Many people assume that global warming only occurs in places miles away and essentially can't harm them. However, Max Schulz, a director of the Center for Energy Policy, asserts that this state is experiencing the "saddest agricultural saga since the Depression-era Dust Bowl", as severe droughts grip California, hurting the state's economic existence as America's major source of agricultural products. More importantly, due to the gradual warming of the seas, storms of greater size and force have taken countless lives, like Hurricane Katrina, which demolished New Orleans. If nothing is done to hold back the prodigious force of global warming, it will continue to infiltrate nations and leave vast amounts of land and people ravaged with desolation.

A number of solutions in abridging the effects of global warming lie at an individual level. One could merely make minor adjustments to his everyday lifestyle, like cut his shower time in half to save water, carpool and reduce the amount of fuel use, or even use energy-efficient light bulbs. The federal government could also provide tax breaks for individuals who make dramatic adjustments to their lives by setting up solar panels in their homes, or converting their vehicles to operate on biodiesel fuel.

Although these efforts are ways to hold back the hand of global warming, the best solution is a cap-and-trade policy in which the federal government establishes a quota on the amount of carbon dioxide that can be released into the atmosphere and issue fees for going over the limit. By restricting the amount of carbon emissions which corporations and fossil fuel producing factories expel, this policy could make greater strides to heal the environment and revolutionize the energy sector.

A cap-and-trade policy would help abate the rise of sea levels. As mentioned earlier, Greenland's ice is dissolving at a fast rate, but Greenland is not the only area experiencing this dramatic shift in ice composition. According to Lonnie G. Thompson, a glaciologist at Ohio State University a decline in "ice atop Mount Kilimanjaro" of more than twenty-six percent has been "paralleled" by "retreats in ice fields" located in "Africa, South America, Indonesia and the Himalayas" (Bhanoo A.6). The rapid dissolution found amongst these various bodies of ice is an inescapable reality and an indication of the future rise of sea levels, as it's unlikely that this melt-water will evaporate at the same speed it is produced.

The Intergovernmental Panel on Climate Change (IPCC) attributes the "rise in global temperatures" and the consequential glacial melting, to the combustion of "human-generated greenhouse gases" (Woodard 30). The emission of fossil fuels into the atmosphere results from a number of actions including driving a car that operates on gas, using gas to heat up one's home, and more notably, the industrial sector's combustion of carbon dioxide. Many are probably skeptical about believing that the actions of the United States alone could significantly help combat the immense issue of glacial disintegration. According to the Pew Center on Global Climate Change, America is the second largest "greenhouse gas emitter," releasing 1.9 billion tons of carbon every year (qtd in Woodard 41). If a cap-and-trade policy was enforced on the American industrial sector, an undeniable stride towards improving the environment would take place. More importantly, considering how America is a superpower exerting great influence on the global community, any changes made in the environmental infrastructure would be met with similar actions of ecological reform across the globe.

A cap-and-trade policy would also improve air quality. According to the Energy Information Administration, in 2007 the industrial sector discharged 1.6 million tons of carbon into the atmosphere ("Official Energy"). Restraining this astonishing amount of pollution would greatly benefit society, as the releasing of noxious gases contaminates the air we breathe, causing asthma, and weakening the immune system. Opponents of cap-and-trade initiatives say that such a policy is useless in curbing air pollution as the Environmental Protection Agency reports that transportation produces seventy percent of the 158 million tons of air pollution in the United States (Cooper 980). This is an excellent assertion since the initial response to restraining air pollution would be to reform the top ranking polluter.

When we analyze the causes of air pollution, a cap-and-trade policy is the best option. Rather than target individuals who own gas consuming cars, this policy instead would target the companies that produce fossil fuels. By restricting the amount of carbon factories can combust, the federal government would restrict their ability to produce fuels, which would decrease the availability of gas. Basic economic principles dictate that, as the supply of gas decreases, the price of this product will increase as a way for the gas industry to maintain a profit. Although in the short term, price increases on gas will have little impact on the demand for gas, in the long term, (for instance two to five years) demand for gas and petroleum will decline as consumers will have a greater window of time to adapt to the drastic increases of gas prices. In retrospect, we have already seen these economic actions take place as more people are saving money to buy electric cars, and are converting their vehicles to function on common household commodities like cooking oil and water.

As we take a look at the impact a cap-and-trade policy would have on the industrial structure, its consequential increase of carbon prices will improve the economy. Those who challenge the cap-and-trade alternative note that the current recession does not create the necessary atmosphere for a massive overhaul of the industrial sector. This is a great argument, as the American Congressional Budget Office predicts that the increase in carbon prices brought on by establishing carbon emission quotas will lead to job losses and lower wages for people working in "carbon-intensive industries" (United States 10). Evidently, unemployment and the resulting decrease in productivity and profit is not the way to guide America out of the depths of recession. In contrast, Henrik Hasselknippe, global carbon services director for Point Carbon, acknowledges that as cap-and-trade regulations allow companies to create solutions and alternatives in dealing with the "limit" placed on carbon "emissions," an "infrastructure" is established which enables "capital for long term investments" (Weeks 299). With higher prices on carbon, companies would have a financial incentive and obligation to produce new, cleaner energy sources if they want to maintain a progressive financially secure corporation. When we consider the process of creating new renewable energy sources, this tremendous endeavor will require the hiring of scientists and engineers to create and manufacture innovations in energy, and workers to carry their visions. Cap-and-trade restrictions can lead to the creation of new eco-friendly jobs, which essentially is a tremendous improvement for the American economy as more jobs mean more productivity and greater profit.

A cap-and-trade policy should be established in America because it can maximize this country's ability to help combat the horrors of global warming such as a rise in sea level, by shedding light on one of the biggest culprits of the climate crisis—companies and factories which produce and expel carbon dioxide into the atmosphere. The cap-and-trade alternative also holds the industrial sector accountable for their failure to consider their impact on the environment as they pursue the capitalistic goal of wealth and success. More importantly, cap-and-trade policies force the industrial structure to release themselves from indifference, to understand the progressive unraveling of nature, and to take action to revolutionize the energy field. Under a cap-and-trade policy, companies will decrease carbon emissions and utilize technology to create new energy sources, to help slow down the gradual deterioration of the ice caps, to improve air quality, and force America to understand the flawed practice of fossil fuel use. Ultimately the Earth continues to struggle with the burden humanity has imposed. Now is not the time to look away with fear as another hurricane claims more lives or turn the other cheek with apathy as the welfare of another species is placed in perilous jeopardy. As a race of people wandering through the new terrain of another millennium, it is our obligation to preserve this world for ourselves and the generations after us.

WORKS CITED

Banhoo, Sindhya N. "Mt. Kilimanjaro's Ice Cap Continues Its Rapid Retreat, but the Cause Is Debated." *New York Times* 3 Nov. 2009: A6. *ProQuest Newsstand.* Web. 4 Dec. 2009.

Cooper, Mary H. "Air Pollution Conflict." *CQ Researcher.* 40.13. (2003): 965–988. Web. 8 Nov. 2009.

Faris, Stephan. *Forecast.* New York: Henry Holt and Co., 2009. Print.

Michaels, Patrick J. and Robert C. Balling. *Climate of Extremes: Global Warming Science They Don't Want You to Know.* Washington: Cato Institute, 2009. Print.

"Official Energy Statistics from the U.S. Government." Energy Information Administration, Washington. Web. 10 Nov. 2009.

Schulz, Max. "Emptying Reservoirs in the Middle of a Drought." *American Spectator* 42.7 (2009): 18–22. Print.

United States Congress. *An Evaluation of Cap-and-Trade Programs for Reducing U.S. Carbon Emissions.* Washington: U.S. Government Printing Office, 2001. Print.

Weeks, Jennifer. "Carbon Trading." *CQ Researcher.* 11.2. (2008): 295–320. Web. 8 Nov.2009.

Woodard, Colin. "Curbing Climate Change." *CQ Researcher.* 1.2. (2007): 27–50. Web. 8 Nov 2009.

IMMIGRATION AND SECURITY

"Immigration, legal and illegal alike, has been
a tool to increase the population of America.
A higher population correlates with the circulation of money."

—KAITLIN SMITH

THE PRICE PAID FOR SECURITY

Ani Ter-Nshanian

Instructor: Jo Anna Bashforth

What price should we be willing to pay for security? That is, how much of our privacy and how many of our constitutionally guaranteed civil rights should we be willing to trade for our safety?

The experience I had with writing this essay was, personally, a good one in that it helped to open my eyes to things I did not know could occur during times of war. After reading all of the sources, I realized that even though people were citizens, they were being persecuted by their own government, and worst of all it was done through the violation of these citizens' rights. As soon as I saw what the essay question was asking, I knew in my heart that I had to pick the side of the citizens who were only guilty of their race. The reason why I was inspired to write this essay was because it helped me to see that every citizen of this country has to know the rights they are entitled to; so just in case the government does violate those rights, they will be aware of it. Therefore, they will not give up their rights and privacy very easily in exchange for security.

No matter who you are, as a citizen of the United States, you are entitled to the protections guaranteed to you by the Constitution. As part of a democratic nation, citizens have the right to speak up and protest against actions of the government they see as unjust. However, history has shown that in times of war, citizens have not been hesitant in taking these rights lightly and essentially giving them up to government control in exchange for safety. When we are putting protection in the hands of the government, we also have to be aware of the fact that they can take our rights for granted. In times of war, American citizens should be aware of the balance between privacy and civil rights, calculating how much they are willing to trade off for safety, because that analysis can eventually determine how far the government should go to protect its citizens.

A major example of the U.S. government's violation of American citizens' civil rights was the internment of Japanese-Americans by President Roosevelt after the 1941 attacks on Pearl Harbor. In "Why Liberties Suffer in Wartime," McCullagh mentions that Executive Order 9066 allowed the military to remove Japanese-Americans from the U.S. west coast. At the time, that area was seen as being in danger to attack with fears that Japanese-Americans would aid the Japanese war effort. However, this did not justify the government taking away the property of their citizens, and confining them in small camps, not to mention making them work in harsh conditions with little pay (Shishima). The government did not only overstep its boundaries, but they also took away most of the vital rights that Japanese-Americans were entitled to as citizens. In the aftermath of Pearl Harbor, while searching for possible threats to the nation, the government should have gone after only people who posed a threat, rather than taking away the rights of all Japanese-Americans.

Decades later during the Bush administration's "war on terror," many Americans believed that the government had overstepped its boundaries, while also putting the rights of citizens at risk. "...the Bush administration is writing the system of checks and balances out of the Constitution by placing the president's military powers above the civil authority of all three branches of the government" (Richey and Feldmann 1). The Bush administration believed that the battlefield for the war was in America; so they detained "enemy combatants" during that time. However, this led many Americans to believe that the government was violating citizens' civil rights. According to Justice Sandra Day O'Connor, "A state of war is not a blank check for the president when it comes to the rights of the nation's citizens" (Richey and Feldmann 2). The argument that Justice O'Connor is trying to make is that the suffering the executive branch was inflicting on prisoners was unjust. The "enemy combatants" were not allowed access to most of their basic rights stated in the Constitution so they can prove their innocence. "Why Liberty Suffers in Wartime," warns us that "We need to ensure that actions by our government uphold the principles of a democratic society, accountable government and international law, and that all decisions are taken in a manner consistent with the Constitution" (McCullagh 538). In times of terror, while the government investigates its own citizens, people fear speaking up because they are afraid they might get into trouble. But the people need to be aware of the fact that there is not only an executive branch, but three branches that must check one another to protect our rights. The United States government was built on the system of check and balances, a system set up so that citizens would not be manipulated or taken advantage of by any one branch of government.

The worst part is that the Bush administration was still trying to add more legislation to the Patriot Act, in 2002. According to the *Minnesota Daily*, citizens should be aware of their rights so that they will not give them up so easily. However, if this is to occur, then the judicial branch will assure that citizens get some protection through the system of checks and balances. In "Privacy, Civil Rights Infringements Multiply After Sept.11," U.S. District Court Judge Gladys Kessler's decision is cited on the executive's withholding of names after September 11, saying "The first priority of the judicial branch must be to ensure that our government always operates within the statutory and constitutional constraints, which distinguish a democracy from a dictatorship" (Staff 543). In this decision, Kessler gave the government fifteen days to discharge the names from the "war on terrorism" investigation. In response to the executive branch's overstepping of its boundaries, the judicial branch took over. When citizens do not advocate protecting their constitutionally guaranteed rights, those rights could be put at risk, but most importantly they can be overlooked and taken advantage of. This is when citizens should see that the judicial branch has to fight for their rights against the executive branch when it crosses those boundaries.

The Bush administration used racial profiling against its own citizens. In "Rower with Muslim Name is an All-American Suspect," Berkow covers the story of an African-American member of the U.S. Olympic rowing team who was profiled a terror suspect due to his Muslim-sounding name. The police officer told Abdullah, the rower on an American team, that the reason they stopped him from flying was because anyone with a common Muslim name had to be checked to see if they were on a terror list (559). In his situation, Abdullah understood that the government was concerned, but the ironic part was that Abdullah was an African-American Catholic with a Muslim name. In a similar manner, the article "Hundreds are Detained After Visits to INS" points out "[t]hese are people who have voluntarily gone. If they had anything to with terrorism, they wouldn't have gone" (Garvey, Groves, Weinstein 1). In fact, in the wake of 9/11, the Los Angeles Immigration Naturalization Service (INS) called Middle Eastern men and boys for a special registration program. However, the INS ended up jailing the majority of these immigrants due to their ethnicity. The lawyer argued that they would not have cooperated with the orders if they were a part of the terrorist plot; he also mentioned that they had done nothing wrong. In the United States Constitution there is an equality clause that essentially says all American citizens are created equal regardless of gender and race. The actions of the government and the INS were wrong because they explicitly violated citizens' rights by racially profiling them. Most of them came to the United States for the freedom and democracy and the rights stated in the Constitution, but when it counted, those rights were taken away.

Only when the government has "probable cause" should it be acceptable for them to "violate" their citizens' constitutional rights in the name of the "greater good". For example, written in a pre-9/11 world, MonDesire describes her reaction to a strip search done on her by U.S. Customs agents because of her race. She claims "...there's something chilling about a federal policy where law-abiding citizens are forced to disrobe, detained without counsel, subjected to intrusive body cavity searches..." (525). MonDesire talks about how uncomfortable it felt to be searched just because of her skin color. In cases like these, the government has no "probable cause" or evidence to justify their searches.

For example, in the Patriot Act's Section 215 is the provision that allows the FBI and other government agencies to get records about a person without showing "probable cause" that the person did anything wrong (Richey and Feldmann 4). Many Middle Eastern citizens were infuriated by this provision, so they filed a lawsuit against it saying that it violated their privacy, freedom of speech, and right to due-process. This is not the only problem; Section 215 also has a secrecy rule so that the accused do not know if their rights are actually being violated. This makes it harder for the victims to fight back, especially when they feel they are being watched. The government, once again, took advantage of their boundaries by accusing American residents of things they could not prove. Due to these problems, the legislative branch later took action, again, by proposing changes to the provisions in the Patriot Act, and getting them approved with a majority vote. These amendments to the act gave detainees the right to sue and challenge accusations in U.S. courts (Richey 1). This scenario shows that American citizens can protest against government actions, and get their way because the Constitution allows them to.

When the government has reason to believe someone has done something illegal, then they should be able to have access to that person's documents. For example, business reporter Heather Green became concerned that "after September 11, it's only natural that the nation would search for ways to increase its security. But law enforcement has overstepped its boundaries of acceptable surveillance of Americans in the past" (526). This overreaching of power, especially through wiretapping, affected what information intelligence agencies could gather and the investigations they could do because it has more control. Americans have to be aware of the kinds of surveillance tactics used by government agencies because they can think they are innocent, but the government could have reason to believe they are guilty. In "Databases and Security vs. Privacy," Green mentions that "…Americans need to…realize that, in the interest of security, law-enforcement and intelligence agencies are likely to start beefing up their databases on citizens" (525). Even though national agencies are not allowed to share information with one-another, security officials alone view databases as a major weapon in the war on terrorism. An alternative proposed in Green's article is that America can adopt a national identity card system. Maybe this option will be the tradeoff between being less anonymous for more security, as Dershowitz mentions in his articles "Why Fear National ID Cards?" (16). This way, Americans will not be giving up their right to privacy completely.

The government should have concrete facts, not just accusations in pursuing a terrorist, because it can lead to problems. In "A Fuzzy Fingerprint Leaves a Lasting Mark," a false accusation left a man and his family wondering if they can ever call their residence "home" again (Tizon 1-4). The FBI had made a false accusation that Brandon Mayfield was involved in a terrorist attack in Spain. But the evidence later showed that Mayfield had not left the country for many years and the FBI had misread the fingerprint. Later, the FBI apologized to the Mayfield family; however, Mayfield felt that the apology did not fix his life after the violation of his civil liberties. He still suspects that they will keep investigating him. In many cases, the government uses its powers to an extent that is unacceptable; therefore, citizens should be weary of this and protect their rights.

Some wonder whether citizens are still aware of their rights and whether this awareness should determine their rights to privacy and security. Citizens for privacy and civil rights would maintain the Constitution and the system of checks and balances. However, citizens who are willing to give up liberties in the place of "security" would say that the government is constitutionally right in taking away the rights of citizens. According to Charen, "…the war powers of the presidency, long respected by the courts, permit special action in the case of war" (541). She tries to persuade citizens that few people would prefer privacy in the place of protecting American citizens. In the closing statement, Charen gives two options to her readers: "If we err on the side of civil liberties instead of on the side of security, hundreds of thousands or millions of Americans could die. If we err on the side of security, many people will be inconvenienced and a few individuals may be wrongly imprisoned for some time" (Charen 541).

Additionally, she uses statements that over-exaggerate her point of choosing security over privacy. She says that millions of Americans can die if we do not choose security; however, many Americans did die on September 11, 2001. It is doubtful that the terrorists would attack again since they were under strict watch. Also, she does not state who will decide on how much of our privacy will be given up and how long that some time will be. During the "war on terror," Charen's statement would have seemed logical; on the other hand, the government can use tactics that would not step over their boundaries. And they did; most of the people had to fight hard to be able to have their constitutionally guaranteed right to trial after being imprisoned. In giving up civil liberties, citizens should be wary of how much the government is violating and how much they are truly protecting.

Times of terror should be the most vital time for American citizens to advocate for their rights stated in the United States Constitution. When citizens feel that their rights are being violated, they have the right to speak up for them. Also, when they feel like their privacy is being intruded upon, they can also fight for that because the judicial branch approved their right to privacy long ago. The more aware citizens are of their civil liberties, the less easy it will be for them to give up those rights to the government in exchange for security, since security is not always defined clearly in times of war. Americans should be aware of how many of their rights and how much of their privacy they are willing to give up, because it will change the outcome of how far the government will go to protect them, by essentially taking away their rights.

Works Cited

Berkow, Ira. "Rower with Muslim Name Is an All-American Suspect." *New York Times,* 21 February 2003. Rpt. in *Everything's an Argument.* 3rd ed. Eds. Andrea A. Lunsford, John J. Rusziewicz, and Keith Walters. Boston: Bedford/St. Martin's, 2004. 559–562. Print.

Charen, Mona. "We Should Relinquish Some Liberty in Exchange for Security." *Creators Syndicate,* 25 Nov. 2002. Rpt. in *Everything's an Argument.* 3rd ed. Eds. Andrea A. Lunsford, John J. Rusziewicz, and Keith Walters. Boston: Bedford/St. Martin's, 2004. 540–542. Print.

Dershowitz, Alan. "Why Fear National ID Cards?" *New York Times,* 13 Oct. 2001. Rpt. in *Everything's an Argument.* 3rd ed. Eds. Andrea A. Lunsford, John J. Rusziewicz, and Keith Walters. Boston: Bedford/St. Martin's, 2004. 556–557. Print.

Garvey, Megan, Groves, Martha, and Weinstein, Henry. "Hundreds Are Detained After Visits to INS." *LATimes.com.* 19 Dec. 2002. Web. 23 Aug. 2005. 1–3. Print.

Green, Heather. "Databases and Security vs. Privacy." *Business Week,* Oct. 2002. Rpt. in *The Informed Argument.* 6th ed. Eds. Robert P. Yagelski, and Robert K. Miller. MA: Thomson Wadsworth, 2004. 524–526. Print.

McCullagh, Declan. "Why Liberty Suffers in Wartime." *Wired News,* Sept. 2001. Rpt. In *Everything's an Argument.* 3rd ed. Eds. Andrea A. Lunsford, John J. Rusziewicz, and Keith Walters. Boston: Bedford/St. Martin's, 2004. 535–539.

MonDesire, Daria. "Stripped of More Than My Clothes." *USA Today,* April 1999. Rpt. in *Everything's an Argument.* 3rd ed. Eds. Andrea A. Lunsford, John J. Rusziewicz, and Keith Walters. Boston: Bedford/St. Martin's, 2004. 525–526. Print.

"Privacy, Civil Rights Infringements Multiply After Sept. 11." Editorial. *Minnesota Daily,* 5 Aug. 2002. Rpt. in *Everything's an Argument.* 3rd ed. Eds. Andrea A. Lunsford, John J. Rusziewicz, and Keith Walters. Boston: Bedford/St. Martin's, 2004. 543–544. Print.

Richey, Warren. "Terror detainees win right to sue." *CSMonitor.com* 29 June 2004. Web. 27 Dec. 2004. 1–3.

Richey, Warren, and Feldmann, Linda. "Has post-9/11 dragnet gone too far?" *CSMonitor.com* 12 Sept. 2003. Web. 27 Dec. 2004. 1–8.

Shishima, Bill. Personal Interview. 1 October 2009.

Tizon, Alex T. "A Fuzzy Fingerprint Leaves a Lasting Mark." *LATimes.com* 29 May 2004. Web. 7 Jan. 2005.

THE IMMIGRATION SOLUTION
Kaitlin Smith

Instructor: Katie McFaddin Christolear

Choose a specific social, economic, political, civic, or environmental issue that concerns you and justify your own stance on the issue.

In a country made up of immigrants, one would assume that they would be forever welcome. Unfortunately, in America, that is not the case. In 1986, an amnesty was granted for all illegal immigrants residing in America. In other words, a pardon was given to all offenders or law breakers who were living in the country without documentation. The benefits from such an act were immeasurable at the time; even today, an amnesty could work to solve some of our country's more pressing problems such as the economic recession. But alas, the process of becoming an American citizen is treacherous. Aside from the rules and regulations that must be meticulously followed to gain citizenship, the time it takes to be processed in the system is borderline ridiculous. The reasons for this are understandable yet inexcusable. After the 9/11 terrorist attacks, America severely tightened its security and made it even more difficult to become a citizen by making the process even more time consuming. If our country hopes to remain a powerful player in the foreign market and rid itself of the economic recession, it would be in the country's best interest to grant an amnesty for all illegal immigrants residing on American soil.

Two hundred years ago, an immigrant needed to be a permanent resident of America in order to be eligible for citizenship, nothing more or less. Less than a decade later the residential requirement turned into five years, and during the second year a declaration of intention to seek citizenship had to be filed as well. Three years later, it became a requirement for immigrants to reside and work in America for fourteen years before they could apply for naturalization. Since then, the requirements for citizenship have been set back to a five-year residency. As good as those five years may seem in comparison to the fourteen year requirement, the fine print for what constitutes an American residency during the five years is confusing for anyone, let alone to a foreigner who most likely does not speak or understand English well enough to follow such rules.

In addition to the residency requirement, immigrants must apply and receive a Green Card, or proof of residency. Acquiring a Green Card is tedious. According to a National webpage, if you do not have a job, work visa, a relative who is a citizen, a spouse who is a citizen, or adoptive parents who are citizens, then you only have two other methods to receive a Green Card. The first of which is to win the Green Card lottery. Specifically, fifty thousand Green Cards are given to random applicants once a year. Interestingly enough, this lottery does not apply to Canadian or Mexican immigrants, despite the fact that these two countries not only share a border with America, but the majority of immigration to America over the years has been from these places. Another method is a classic American one: all a prospective American citizen needs to do is buy the informational application guide and sail through the rest of the process. If only it were as simple as they make it seem. Therefore, if one desires citizenship and is not eligible to receive a Green

Card through the standard requirements, then all one must do is purchase the application guide for almost one hundred dollars. This is in addition to the fact that since one is an illegal immigrant, one cannot have a job - at least not legally. Since one does not have a job, then one has no money, and if one has no money, then one cannot purchase the application guide necessary to figure out how else one can be eligible for a Green Card ("USCIS Citizenship"). Without the guide, one has no other options. At the end of the day, options are few, and the situation becomes hopeless. Nevertheless, the opportunities America seems to present for these immigrants makes the struggles worth it. The dreams that can come true prevail, the determination that immigrants have to succeed and have a better life triumphs over any struggle that may occur in the process. Having a chance to have the best and happiest life possible is something that every single person in the world should have. The blessings and opportunities America presents should be available to anyone who feels capable of taking on the challenge.

Although it may be a long awaited dream to become a citizen, the process of getting there is far too tedious, time consuming, and unfair to the applicants. What should be a fair process with periodic loads of paperwork and waiting in long lines, like any other American has to do when dealing with governmental issues, becomes a market place for products and commercialization. Yet the trials do not cease, after receiving a Green Card, multiple other procedures must be followed carefully. In addition to the challenge of being a stranger on American soil, foreigners are expected to understand and follow procedures of the complex legal system, a system that average Americans struggle with. Regardless of the disadvantages, illegal immigrants still reside in America, they still do undocumented work and are employed illegally, and they still buy American goods and utilize American services. Illegal immigrants have entire families and homes and cars, everything a regular citizen has. And America cannot give these immigrants citizenship because of paperwork and the overwhelming amount of applicants. These people do not just need citizenship, they deserve it.

After the terrorist attacks on September 11, 2001, our country was devastated and deeply wounded. What had seemed like an impenetrable powerhouse kingdom was left as a vulnerable madhouse. America re-evaluated itself. It cranked up its security measures and began looking for someone to blame. While efforts were being made to find and punish the foreign offender behind the attack, many Muslims and Arabs residing on American soil were heckled and condemned. Hundreds of these innocent people were investigated, tried, criticized and questioned, simply because of their country of origin. Whether it is by the government or by the American people and whether the victims are citizens or not, a stigma was created for all those *resembling* the terrorists. After 9/11, legislation was passed that made unauthorized entry into the United States an aggravated felony. In addition, a bill called Border Protection, Anti-terrorism, and Illegal Immigration Control Act of 2005 was passed. This legislation basically tightens security, increases border patrol, summarizes harsher punishment, and makes coming into and leaving America almost impossible for illegal immigrants. Aside from the legality of the situation, remittances or money sent from families in America to families in foreign countries (in this case, Mexico), have dropped drastically. Governmental aid for immigrants became extremely unavailable. In its entirety, the aftermath of 9/11 could have been handled in a much better way. Instead of spending valuable money on better security measures for threatening countries abroad, it was spent on hiring more men to patrol the Mexican border and it was spent on building fences to keep such people out. As if our country's biggest worry was keeping out the immigrants from Mexico who were no more of a threat than any ordinary citizen, when in reality all these immigrants from Mexico do is contribute to the flow of money in American economy (US Immigration History).

After a prosperous economic era, America began to slip on the worldwide scale. The slip turned into quite a fall and the country landed in a recession. Aside from a loss of economic growth, unemployment has multiplied, immigration has dramatically dropped, and any currency remaining in the system has dried up and ceased flowing. According to "The Crunch Time," an article in the *Economist:*

> As migrant workers suffer in America—general unemployment is over 7%, a 16-year-high, with Hispanic workers hit especially--the message sent home is 'don't come'. It has been received clear enough, for now. A study of 120,000 Mexican households published in November showed emigration (almost entirely to America) had slumped by 42% from two years earlier. Border arrests have fallen equally fast. The value of remittances has also tumbled, says Mexico's central bank. ("The People Crunch")

Now the economy is at a standstill. Small changes are being made by the government. Different policies and possible solutions are being offered and considered; few are successful. Immigration, legal and illegal alike, has been a tool to increase the population of America. A higher population correlates with the circulation of money. A more populous location will have more money flowing and assisting an economy than a location with a lower population.

Some may argue that a recession will cause our country to further suffer. Immigration increases job competition, taxes could rise. Such struggles are normal in young and developing countries, especially in a country where part of its economic recession can be traced to the unequal distribution of income in society. It is common knowledge among the working world that the majority of the country's wealth resides among the upper classes. The way for that money to make its way back into the system is to increase the lower and middle classes of society and slowly shrink the upper class. Immigrants do not come to America for a first class lifestyle. They come to struggle for a better life. By struggling and contributing to the American system, the middle and lower classes become larger. Taxes may rise, but if they rise for the lower classes, then they rise for the upper class as well. In the long run, more sacrifices are made on the part of the upper class. Through increased taxes, the money will eventually redistribute itself and America may regain its stability and rise once more as a threatening world power.

In the article "Five Hot Ideas for Today's Economy," Anne Fisher states that "The U.S., in effect, is losing the competition for skilled workers in the immigration market." Unfortunately, in the 9/11 aftermath and overly restrictive citizenship procedures, America has ceased to be a prosperous country. In the midst of restraining immigration and throwing away tax dollars on ineffective and pointless rules that discourage and complicate coming to this country, America crept off of the world meter. The agony from the recession can be easily relieved by an amnesty. Not only will it increase immigration, but the power of the entire country will rise as well. With power in increased numbers, America can once more have a successful economy. An amnesty would equalize all inhabitants of this nation. Once everyone is a citizen, everyone will have a chance to live a happy life.

Works Cited

Diner, Hasia. "Immigration and U.S. History." *America—Engaging the World—America. gov.* U.S. Department of State, 13 Feb. 2008. Web. 20 Nov. 2009.

Fisher, Anne B. "Five Hot Ideas For Today's Economy." *Fortune* 128.9 (1993): 112–121. *Academic Search Elite.* EBSCO. Web. 26 Nov. 2009.

"The People Crunch." *Economist* 390.8614 (2009): 58–60. *Academic Search Elite.* EBSCO. Web. 26 Nov. 2009.

"US immigration History." *American Immigration—USCIS and Visa Information.* RapidImmigration. Web. 20 Nov. 2009.

"USCIS - Citizenship." *USCIS Home Page.* Spring 2003. Web. 20 Nov. 2009.

BORDER PATROL AND IMMIGRATION
Cana Phylicia Reyes

Instructor: Rebecca Lawson

Analyze a civic issue pertaining to a city or community.

I decided to do my paper on the U.S.–Mexico border and illegal immigration because of the controversy surrounding it. Being an immigrant myself, the topic was very relatable. I was unsure of which side to take, whether or not it is practical for the government to spend millions of dollars annually on border improvement. However, after much research, I chose a side, researched evidence, and argued against the investment of government money on the southern border.

As of August 2009, U.S. Border Patrol estimates that about 378 immigrants have perished in an attempt to cross the border. This tally will surpass the previous year's estimate of 390 deaths by the end of the fiscal year. Regulation the United States' southern border to Mexico is a delicate and controversial issue. Although logic would suggest that the recent economic downturn and "improved" border security would slow down illegal immigration, the increased death among immigrants disproves this argument. Hundreds of hopeful undocumented aliens continue to attempt and, most of the time, die in failure to cross the border. Illegal immigration will always be an issue in our society. Millions of dollars are spent annually to improve fences, hire patrol agents, and install hidden cameras in order to reduce the flow of illegal immigrants from south of the border. However, is it really worth it to spend this much money on something that is clearly ineffective and unfruitful? Tighter border control does not result in improved border protection. Rather, it results a more dangerous barrier that clearly does not stop immigrants from attempting to pass them. The millions of dollars spent yearly to improve borders increase national security and control illegal immigration is ineffective and only puts hundreds of human lives in danger. Instead of spending this bulk of money on something that is fruitless and evidently costly to human lives, it should be used to fund the legal migration of immigrants to the United States.

The economic recession affects people globally, especially to those with fewer resources. This is especially the case for poor immigrants from south of the border. As a result, it is more essential than ever to move to a more developed country and try their fortunes there instead of staying in their native country and be driven deeper into poverty. Whether or not tighter border security is effective, nothing can stop a person from attempting to move his or her family to a place of better opportunity. By interviewing 4,000 illegal immigrants and potential migrants, Wayne Cornelius, a US San Diego director for the Center for Comparative Immigration, concluded that "The existing border fortifications do not keep undocumented immigrants from the US…the success rate on the second or third try [of cross the border] is upwards of 95 percent" (Wood). In other words, our "tighter" borders do not impede those drastically affected by the global economic recession from crossing our borders. Immigrants will inevitably be pushed to move to the United States, no matter how difficult the obstacle course becomes. The immigrants' intentions are pure and uncorrupt, and they are not threats to national security. The death rate for immigrants from crossing the border does not justify the harmlessness of their intentions.

Triple digit temperatures, drowning in canals, automobile traffic, and murder are the leading causes of illegal immigrant deaths in the United States (Eschbach). In order to increase their chances of getting in the country successfully, immigrants attempt crossing the border at remote locations where security is less strict and border patrol agents are not as pervasive. Since millions of dollars are spent annually to "improve" borders by hiring more patrol agents and installing hidden cameras, immigrants are pushed more than ever to go to extremes so that they can come to the United States. One extreme is to cross the border at the most intense locations such as Arizona's Sonora Desert, where temperatures can reach up to 115 degrees Fahrenheit. The long and arduous walk to civilization ultimately takes a toll on these immigrants' stamina and endurance, and most perish from dehydration or hyperthermia. In Texas, the most prevalent method to cross the border illegally is through the Del Rio River, where an estimated 40 immigrants die yearly from drowning. Some attempt to squeeze through canals and other irrigation systems, hoping it would lead them to the US. Consequently, some drown from the unpredictable flow of water. Immigrants who cross the border through a smuggler are also at risk. A smuggler in Arizona was rescued because the weight of the 19 immigrants busted the tire of his Ford Excursion truck, causing it to lose control. All 20 people were injured (Billeaud). Anti-immigrant citizens situated near these borders shoot at illegal immigrants after they have successfully crossed the border. These statistics are startling, and it is even more surprising to learn that these deaths do not cover the entire scope of the immigrant death rate. It neglects the immigrants whose bodies were never found in the desert or whose bodies have washed away from the canals. The projected death toll of 378 lives as of August 2009 underestimates the reality of the situation.

Immigrants' lack of documentation impedes them from meeting the minimum rights and privileges any American is entitled to in United States. Lacking the proper documents such as a Social Security number and driver's license, they are unable to acquire respectable jobs. As a result, they take blue collar jobs such as janitorial or construction work, the most physical and unskilled form of labors. Because they are undocumented, most employers perceive them as ineligible to qualify for basic labor laws such as an eight-hour work shift or, worse yet, lunch breaks. Most employers do not bother following state laws by not paying their workers the standard minimum wage, knowing that any complaints can lead to deportation. Their lack of legal documentation also prohibits them from joining or forming unions as a counter action to abusive work demands. Consequently, most illegal immigrants stay and endure the unfair demands simply because it puts food on the table (Welch).

Since 2005, the government has spent about $2.4 billion dollars to improve the US-Mexico border and erect more fences to strengthen its effectiveness. An additional $6.5 billion must be expended "to maintain the new fencing over the next 20 years" (Wood). Since the recent economic downfall and tighter border security have done nothing but increase immigrants' death rate, does this imply that the government is spending billions of dollars for an unpractical purpose, otherwise known as border security? How many more lives must perish so that the unreasonable spending would stop? Rather than investing billions of dollars on goals that are clearly ineffective and unrealistic, the government should divert this sum of money to fund the legal migration of aliens in the United States. Legalization is a lengthy and costly process. The government should consider aiding the financially incapable through this by making the fees more affordable and the process less extensive. This could only be done by funding the legalization process for incoming illegal immigrants and the 12 million aliens already in the United States (Welch). Consequently, if more illegal immigrants are legalized, it would become unnecessary for those who were born legal to pay higher taxes and government fees.

Some may argue that illegal immigrants become a source of cheap labor that takes away opportunity from the unemployed in the United States, but this is not always the case, since most unemployed Americans today are middle-class, highly educated people. Due to the economic slump, they most likely got laid off. Therefore, these Americans will not settle for blue collar jobs that pay poorly and demand compromising work hours. Realistically speaking, more American factories would go out of business if cheap, unskilled laborers were removed from the labor market. Some might also argue that illegal aliens' presence cause the American public to pay more taxes and fees. Illegal immigrants' children are in need of welfare and other government aids. In emergencies, hospitals cannot deny anyone the right to medical attention. So when uninsured, illegal immigrants are in need of medical intervention, hospitals are forced to give them treatment for a very low, almost free, price. This is unfair for those who have insurance and are paying the standard fee for healthcare. Those inclined to pay taxes because they are legal end up paying extra for the untaxed, illegal immigrants. If the government redirected the money spent on border security to fund legal migration, this problem could be avoided. Not only would illegal immigrants have the ability to acquire better jobs that pay more fairly, they would also pay taxes like any other American citizen. It is important to consider the circumstances these immigrants underwent in the "migrating" process as well as their everyday lifestyles. Even if they were able to pay taxes and have medical insurance, their lack of legal documentation would prohibit them from acquiring higher jobs and would therefore still be unable to sustain payments given their work conditions and salaries.

Although more money is expended to increase border security and fence improvements, the recent global economic downturn has enticed illegal immigrants to migrate to the United States more than ever because of the poverty they experience at home. Tighter border security is forcing immigrants to change their crossing points from urban areas to more remote deserts. Unfortunately, some die in this process as a result of hunger or dehydration. Their undocumented status in the United States subjects them to the worst of work conditions and salary. Though some may argue that illegal immigrants provide nothing but more headache for America, they should consider how little of the population is willing to take the jobs immigrants do, and the services they provide because they take these positions. Rather than using the billions of dollars annually for the "improvement" of our borders, the government should instead use it to fund the legalization of illegal aliens in the country.

WORKS CITED

Billeaud, Jacques. "2009 Deaths Likely to Exceed 2008 Total." *US Customs and Border Protection. America's Intelligence Wire.* 2 Oct. 2009. Web. 13 Nov. 2009.

Esbach, Karl. "Death at the Border." *International Migration Review.* 33 (1999): 430–54. Web. 13 Nov. 2009.

Von Drehle, David. "A New Line in the Sand." *New York Times.* 171.26(2008): 28. Web. 13 Nov. 2009.

Welch, Jack. "Immigration: A Reality Check." *Business Week.* 25 Feb. 2008. 4072(2008): 96. Web. 23 Nov. 2009.

Wood, Daniel. "Billions for a US-Mexico Border Fence, But is it Doing Any Good?" *The Christian Science Monitor.* 19 Sept. 2 (2009). Web 24 Nov. 2009.

HEALTH

"I remember playing many recreational activities such as dodge ball, and all I learned from it was how to throw objects at people. In some cases, this skill may actually come in handy, but it is not necessarily teaching the values of engaging in physical activity."

—DANIEL NGUYEN

COLD, HUNGRY, AND HOMELESS: A SECOND CHANCE
FOR THE FORGOTTEN PEOPLE
Arthur Azatyan

Instructor: Rachael Jordan

Write an essay that takes a stand on an arguable issue and supports its position through the use of strong description and evidence, real and/or likely examples, clear establishment of terms, acknowledgement and analysis of counterarguments, and careful reasoning. You need to analyze the issue and present your position by appealing to credibility/character (ethos), emotions/values (pathos), and logic (logos).

Writing this essay on homelessness was the greatest challenge I faced in English 155; it is the culmination of all that I have learned during the course and I think is the best representation of my writing skills. The actual assignment itself was a very broad one; it was simply to pick a theme from The Soloist *and defend my opinion on it by using strong arguments and rebut possible counterarguments through supportive evidence. I chose the topic of homelessness, but I soon realized it was far too general, and so I had to rewrite it with a focus on homelessness in the United States and presented a proposition that could possibly end it. Although I ended up writing something different than what I had originally intended, I think it was ultimately for the better and am very proud of the outcome of my paper.*

Poverty and homelessness have plagued the United States since its birth, but within these last few decades it has evolved from a relatively minor nuisance to a national epidemic. Homeless populations are on the rise and pose numerous problems ranging from economic burdens, to safety concerns, to health issues; and communities all across the nation are desperate for a solution. The public is in outrage at how so many hardworking Americans and their families are now victims of homelessness and the reality is finally sinking in that in this crumbling economy, no one is safe. In response to this threat, the federal government, major cities, relief organizations, and even individuals are all scrambling to stabilize and reverse the situation any way they can; but in these dire economic times, resources are falling short, so we must demand for radical government reform like universal health care and rapid re-housing along with putting a much greater emphasis on benevolent community outreach to finally end this cancer to society.

The question is clear: how do we permanently end homelessness on a national level? Yet for many Americans the question is: why should we care? The sad truth is that so many Americans have twisted ideology on homelessness which stems from society's negative stereotyping of homeless people, coupled with their parents' lack of respect for the homeless, which has left an unfortunate impression in their minds since childhood. It is this shroud of misconception and blatant ignorance that is holding this nation back from progress. The huge divide in the public's attitude on homelessness is allowing for the government to take the cheapest route and provide only the bare minimum in assistance or ignore the problem altogether. Yet because they're not taking real steps to solve this problem, the government is inadvertently allowing it to grow in an almost snowball effect to a now estimated "840,000 people homeless in America each day, [and] up to 3 million homeless [each] year" as estimated by the 2003 U.S. Conference of Mayors (Triplett 545). With this outrageous number of homeless people walking the streets everyday, unable to support themselves, and living in unsanitary conditions, it is easy to see how this would cause a huge financial strain on local hospitals, police departments and shelters, all of which are being paid for by federal and state tax dollars. For this reason alone, not even yet taking into account the moral obligations we should adhere to, it is obvious why homelessness is without a doubt a problem *everyone* should be concerned about, because as long as they live in this country, it will ultimately affect them and their families where it hurts most: their pocket books.

Before anyone can propose a solution to the problem of homelessness, it's important to first properly identify who truly makes up the homeless population. The public stereotype of the homeless is old, crazy people who everyone sees begging on the streets, the ones with long, bushy beards who reek of urine and cheap liquor, and who will sadly prefer to beg for change so they can buy some drugs or alcohol rather than put that money to getting their life in order; but it would be a gross mistake to apply this stereotype to all or even most homeless people. The truth is that most homeless people are indeed victims of their circumstances; many do in fact have at least one job and work extremely hard to be able to feed and support themselves and their family, but fall short of affording a place to live.

One such person was my former neighbor whom I had the honor of interviewing about a year ago. She was a single mom who, for the last year, had been raising her child out of her minivan after they had been evicted from their last home because she couldn't pay the rent. Undaunted, she continued working and overcame tremendous adversity to finally obtain a stable career as a florist at a local flower shop and provide a stable home for her child. She described her experience with homelessness as frightening, not knowing what the next day will bring and the chance that her daughter might be taken away from her was a living nightmare. She went on to say that she "was too ashamed to ask anyone for help and none of [her] daughter's friends knew [they] were homeless in fear that someone would call child services and take away the only thing [she] had left" (Conan). It was at this moment of revelation that I abandoned all false stereotypes I had previously accepted of homeless people, and at last understood that homelessness is not a choice, nor is it a fate reserved for the lazy or mentally ill; it is, in fact, a very real and ubiquitous threat looming over the unsuspecting millions who would never imagine they could one day become homeless themselves.

Now knowing who the subjects of this paper really are, it's now time to take action and help those actually trying to escape a life of poverty. The first step in combating this growing epidemic is to lower the cost of living by no longer forcing people to pay for things that should be free. Medical treatment, for example, should not be a privilege reserved for the rich; it should be a birthright shared by everyone. Propositions like universal health care are one way of trying to make this a reality. According to the article "Health-Care Reform," written by Marcia Clemmitt, "one in seven Americans, approximately 45.7 million people, do not have any kind of health care; if so many Americans can't afford health insurance for themselves and their families, what chance do the homeless have to tend to their ailments until it's too late" (Clemmit 701). This lack of preventative healthcare allows diseases or wounds that could so easily have been treated progress to a point that not only drastically jeopardizes the life of the individual, but also costs hospital emergency rooms much more to treat at this stage.

By the government taking the initiative and following through in this proposal, millions of Americans living at or below the poverty line will finally be able to get the medical treatment they need at no cost to them. This will allow families to direct more of their income to sustaining their household and would effectively help prevent them from falling into homelessness in the first place. Critics of this proposal argue that such healthcare reform would result in a tax increase, and unfortunately, yes, this is true; but the benefits drastically outweigh the costs and those critics are forgetting that nothing in this world is free and are failing to take into account the value of a human life.

America was once a world symbol of health and prosperity, but in recent years, it seems that the well-being of its citizens has taken a back seat in its priority list, and so this country and its people have lost sight of "the common good." Daniel Callahan, co-founder of the Hastings Center, a bioethics research institute, and author of "America's Blind Spot" describes the lack of a sense of the common good as the "blind spot" in American healthcare reform. He acknowledges that countries like Canada, the Netherlands, France, and Switzerland "understand a simple point…good public services require adequate funding, and the tax revenue that pays for such services is money well spent" and that in those countries "the common good is considered an important political principle [so] the government takes a more active role: hence their stronger welfare programs (and much lower poverty rates), as well as their universal healthcare systems" (Callahan 13). It's this concept of "money well spent" that critics fail to understand, and it's this selfish mentality and inhumanity to fellow citizens that is allowing for homelessness to run rampant. If everyone stopped being so egocentric, worrying about the small tax hike and looking at the bigger picture, homelessness would certainly be eliminated within our generation and in doing so, would also secure a safer, healthier, and more prosperous future for generations to come.

With all this attention on the federal government and its lack of initiative, it's easy to get carried away pointing fingers and forgetting who the federal government ultimately serves. The state and federal governments are at the whim of the people, and so much of what is mandated is by the citizens. It's only because we don't have a unified voice on the subject that things are not being done. It's *our* responsibility to push these legislations, like healthcare reform, into effect through public outcry and upheaval; we shouldn't sit on our hands and wait for a solution that will never come while millions are dying of hunger and ailments that could have been easily prevented. With that said, it's just as important for communities and even individuals to take the initiative and help the less fortunate in any way they can. One such person was Steve Lopez, a *Los Angeles Times* columnist who stumbled across a homeless man named Nathaniel Anthony Ayers, an extremely gifted musician who was suffering from schizophrenia. Lopez went out of his way to help Ayers turn his life around and show the world his talent; in doing so, he created a lifelong friendship and walked away with a newfound appreciation and respect for someone who could have so easily been mistaken as just another hopeless, homeless man.

No one is expected to go above and beyond like Lopez did and devote nearly every waking hour to help a single person, but there is so much an average person can do to make a huge impact in many people's lives. Things as simple as volunteering in local soup kitchens, donating food and clothing to organizations that dispense them to the needy and even giving spare change to the homeless are all ways that can alleviate the burden of living on the streets. Yet, while these things are admirable acts of kindness, they ultimately do little to help the situation in the long run. The fact of the matter is that those few dollars you may give a homeless person might buy them a burger, but won't buy them a home, won't buy them the surgery they might need, won't get them a job, and definitely won't end their suffering. The only way to offer a permanent solution is to give them an opportunity. That's all they need: just someone to look past their rough exterior and see the person inside, desperate for a second chance.

Many cities that have been impacted by the current recession and have suffered widespread foreclosures are now noticing a sudden upsurge of homeless people in their shelters and struggling to provide for all of them. City officials recognize that their limited resources cannot sustain such huge populations and that the only way this problem can be corrected is by offering self-sustainability and rapid re-housing. That is the only way to break this vicious cycle of poverty and pave the road to recovery for those who truly want it. These cities are guided by a ten-year plan, each plan tailor-made by Philip Mangano, executive director of the federal Interagency Council on Homelessness and nicknamed President Bush's "homeless czar." In his interview with David Neff, chief editor of *Christianity Today,* Mangano says he is convinced that homelessness can be abolished within ten years if cities collaborate with corporations, nonprofit organizations, hospitals, and other parts of the private sector to offer affordable housing and supportive assistance to families who wouldn't be able to afford a home unaided. He rationalizes this by asking, should we "spend $35,000-$150,000 per year on emergency rooms, police, fire, public defenders, and so on for a chronically homeless person? Or should [we] spend $13,000-$25,000 on supportive housing in order to create stability for that person and a trajectory toward self-sufficiency and recovery?" (Neff). It's this concept of self-sustainability and prevention that is the backbone of his campaign, and he is proud to say that it is in fact working. Statistics show that cities merely four years into their ten-years are already seeing results and that "between 2005 and 2007, there was an overall 12 percent decrease in homelessness; the first documented national decrease" (Neff). With these kinds of results, critics have no viable argument against programs like this and there should be no reason why homelessness should persist any longer than it already has. The time is near when the sight of a family living in the streets is a distant memory and this dark chapter in American history can come to a close.

Although the problem has been identified and numerous solutions have been proposed and pushed into effect, the road to recovery is still a long and arduous one. Only through a unified voice can we demand change and only through a unified spirit can we enact it. The United States, which has historically been the greatest advocate of human rights, is now sadly turning a blind eye on millions of its homeless citizens. How can we, in good conscience, stand by as fellow men, women, and children suffer at our doorsteps? If any one of us has called ourselves human, we should stop and think about what constitutes one; it's unfortunate to say that it's this humanity that many of us lack. It's the genuine caring for others, the willingness to help a stranger, and the ability to offer a second chance, that we, as Americans, and better yet, as humans, must develop if we are ever to have hope in undoing this tragedy. It seems I have painted a grim portrait of our society, but it's never too late to right a wrong, and as long as we stand up as one single entity and speak in a single voice, we can undoubtedly put an end to homelessness once and for all.

Works Cited

Callahan, Daniel. "America's Blind Spot." *Commonweal* 136.17 (2009): 13. *MAS Ultra—School Edition*. EBSCO. Web. 27 November 2009.

Clemmitt, Marcia. "Health-Care Reform." *CQ Researcher* 19.29 (2009): 693–716. *CQ Researcher*. Web. 12 November 2009.

Conan, Charlene. Personal Interview. January 2008.

Lopez, Steve. *The Soloist: A Lost Dream, an Unlikely Friendship, and the Redemptive Power of Music*. New York: Berkeley Group, 2008. Print.

Neff, Davi. "Abolishing homelessness in ten years: Philip Mangano, the federal 'homeless czar' says, 'yes we can.'" *Christianity Today*. (May 2009): 52–4. *General OneFile*. Web. 27 November 2009.

Triplett, William. "Ending Homelessness." *CQ Researcher* 14.23 (2004): 541–64. *CQ Public Affairs Collection*. Web. 12 November 2009.

MOVING AWAY FROM SEDENTARY LIFESTYLES
Daniel Nguyen

Instructor: Jessica Morrill

Writer's Choice Persuasive Paper

As a CSUN student in Kinesiology and with aspirations to pursue a profession as an occupational therapist, I find it highly important to promote physical activity among our communities. My goal is to raise awareness among individuals of the benefits of engaging in physical activity daily and to live a healthy lifestyle. This paper allows me to educate, inform, and express these values. Taking action now will help bring you one step closer to a happier and healthier life.

We live in a world filled with many distractions. Some of us may spend most of our time using electronic devices and gadgets, while others take advantage of life's opportunities and explore the various activities and hobbies available to them. Distractions, such as technology, steer us away from living life to the fullest. Our society has developed a serious problem of sedentarism. Consequently, this has led to even more problems, such as obesity. The nation's lack of physical activity and exercise among individuals has created a negative impact on our society. Over the past decade, we have seen a substantial increase in the incidence of obesity among younger generations, and there has never been a more urgent need for action. Many children and young adults get little to no exercise. Action must be taken to promote physical activity in our communities for everyone, especially children.

According to the Educational Resource Information Center, "more than half of U.S. adults do not meet recommended levels of moderate physical activity, and one-fourth engage in no leisure time physical activity at all" (Summerfield). Physical inactivity and lack of exercise are major factors leading to such high rates of obesity. Just to clarify the meaning, "obesity is defined simply as too much body fat" ("Physical Activity in Your Daily Life"). Our type of diets and lifestyles are also contributing factors to consider. "Some of the health hazards carried by obesity include increased mortality rate, high blood pressure, heart disease, and stroke" ("Health Consequences"). So what exactly is physical activity and how can we benefit from it? To put it simply, physical activity is anything that requires one to move around and use energy. An example would be walking or playing basketball. Engaging in daily physical activity offers many benefits ranging from physical to psychological changes. Some of the benefits, which can also be found online through the Centers for Disease Control and Prevention and the American Heart Association websites, include building and maintaining healthy bones, muscles and joints, increased energy expenditure, promoting positive attitudes toward an active lifestyle, increased life expectancy, and decreased risk of cardiovascular disease. There is also evidence that shows physical education may improve academic performance and mental health ("Physical Activity and Health"). These benefits alone are enough incentive to promote physical activity among our communities.

So why is obesity still such a huge problem? One possible reason could be the lack of awareness for the importance of a healthy lifestyle throughout communities, but the reasons could be widely varied due to economic and environmental issues. The environment or community an individual or group resides in may influence their decisions. For example, living in an area or community that lacks sidewalks may affect one's decision on whether or not to walk to a store or work. Communities, homes, and other outside factors such as school and work all have a major impact on our lives. At home, our lifestyles and values are shaped by our family members and the way we live. For instance, a child's inactive lifestyle may have developed through the vast amount of time spent watching television or using the computer. As a child, I remember staying at home playing on my Super Nintendo Gaming System because my parents would always be too busy with work and often my siblings would not want to play with me. Each individual has his or her own starting point in life and just needs to get through all the obstacles in order to reach the finish line. Sometimes, an individual just needs a little push or assistance along the way.

In school, the lack of physical activity among students may be due to the inefficiency of physical education. My personal experiences in school physical education were nowhere near satisfying. It always felt like a resting period or free time because we barely engaged in moderate or vigorous activity. I remember playing many recreational activities such as dodge ball, and all I learned from it was how to throw objects at people. In some cases, this skill may actually come in handy, but it is not necessarily teaching the values of engaging in physical activity. There was really no significance or purpose that taught children the meaning of exercise and staying healthy. In workplaces, it is even more difficult for individuals to get any physical activity since they often lack time or have no opportunity to do so. People often see the workplace as the place to work only and not necessarily to have fun or do other miscellaneous activities.

Examining this topic from a global point of view, it is easy to see a strong positive correlation between physical inactivity and obesity. A goal was set a decade ago by Healthy People 2010 that no more than 15 percent of the population would be obese in 2010. According to the Center for Disease Control and Prevention, data shows that "an estimated 32.7 percent of U.S. adults 20 years and older are overweight, 34.3 percent are obese and 5.9 percent are extremely obese" ("At a Glance"). The number of obese children was reported to have tripled to 17 percent. It was also identified that African-American and Hispanic adults have the highest obesity rates. The increasing number of children becoming overweight and obese is causing a great concern to the public. To further understand this issue and the necessary actions needed to be taken, we must focus on the building blocks of this problem.

As mentioned earlier, there are a variety of factors that influence and shape an individual's life. The environment is just one of those factors, and in order for us to reduce the problems, we need to focus on each individual factor to create an efficient plan or strategy. The environment consists of a variety of sub-factors that influence our decisions and choices. Let me start off with the place individuals spend most of their time: their home. The key to successfully changing an individual's sedentary lifestyle is to start changing daily routines and habits. With the emergence of technology and new trends, our lives have definitely been reshaped and have influenced our decisions and choices in many ways. One way to start change at home is to limit the use of technology and electronic devices. For example, reduce the amount of time spent watching television or using the computer each day. Another suggestion is to try incorporating some sort of physical activity, such as jogging, into daily routines. For individuals who work, try convincing employers to add time for employees to participate in a short physical activity at the workplace. In communities, the key to getting people involved and active is through promoting health and nutrition awareness and encouraging physical activity. This can be achieved by creating neighborhood councils or programs to inform residents about health-related issues and how to get involved in an active lifestyle. A great suggestion I received from one of my peers was to develop neighborhood team sports. I definitely feel this will encourage communities to be active, as well as give everyone the opportunity to meet new people.

Encouraging physical activity among children and youth is highly dependent on schools since children spend a majority of their time there. Through physical education, students have learned the importance of being physically active in their daily lives and gain enjoyment through physical activity. However, as we move on towards the 21st century, the emergence of technology and new trends has changed all of that. Physical education in schools has proved to not be sufficient enough to encourage students to take on an active lifestyle. CDC recommends "children and adolescents should do 60 minutes (1 hour) or more of physical activity each day" ("How much physical activity do children need?"). The general guideline for everyone is a minimum of 30 minutes of moderate physical activity on 5 or more days per week and schools often fail to provide that.

It is my own personal belief that physical education taught in schools is the key to promoting physical activity and to encouraging children to live an active lifestyle. Schools and physical education instructors should keep in mind that they are not only trying to get students to be active during school, but also to enjoy and have fun being physically active throughout their lives. Liane Summerfield suggests in her article that "in addition to being physically active, children need to learn fundamental motor skills and develop health related physical fitness" (Summerfield). Unfortunately, school standards have changed, making physical education less of a priority. According to CDC, "In 2007, 35% of high school students had participated in at least 60 minutes per day of physical activity on 5 or more of the last 7 days, and only 30% attended physical education class daily" ("Healthy Youth!"). It is clearly evident that the role of schools in physical education needs to be reevaluated and constructed in a way so that children are in a supportive and positive environment.

Some would argue that we simply do not have enough money to fund such physical education programs or there is not enough time for physical activity. Those are both plausible arguments. Considering the current economic status, most communities are facing many poverty issues. Increasing physical activity in school curriculum may upset parents who might complain that it takes away time from learning general academic education. There is no definite way to avoid all the expenses of incorporating more physical activity programs; however, there are ways to help alleviate the costs. One option is to use volunteers to teach students. By using volunteers, we can reduce the cost of hiring staff. We can also fundraise and host events. As for lack of time, physical activity should be "considered an excellent investment toward the development of lifetime activity (Ballard and Chase 44). The benefits of physical activity in both short and long term should prove to be a quality investment.

For some time now, we have seen this common pattern of physical activity levels declining in individuals as they grow older; however, it appears it has gotten much worse as more young children are becoming inactive and lazy. There are numerous ways to promote physical activity among individuals. CDC and AHA have already created guidelines and recommendations as to how to get individuals, specifically children, to become physically active. One suggestion mentioned to get students physically active in school is adding "fitness breaks" during class time, where a 5-10 minute break would be used to get students active through activities suggested by physical education instructors. Establishing more physical activity programs and providing opportunities for children to be active has also shown to be effective. For example, creating walking and/or running clubs, or introducing intramural sports or activities may encourage children to participate and become active. Physical activity should be fun for everyone and people just need to experience it.

For anyone experiencing physical inactivity in their lives, the best way to change that would be to reduce the amount of time spent on sedentary activities such as watching television or playing video games. Children, in particular, are most susceptible to physical inactivity due to such sedentary activities, which is why parents should try to be active role-models, encouraging their children to go outside and play and provide other opportunities for increased physical activity. Instead of giving a child a gaming system, one should try giving a basketball or bicycle. Try taking children to environments more suited to physical activity such as public parks or recreation centers. Everyone has a role they can adopt and the opportunity to improve. All of these suggestions and ideas may sound tedious or small, but every step taken to change a lifestyle will create an overall quality of life better for oneself and those around them.

Works Cited

"At-A-Glance." 17 November 1999. *Centers for Disease Control and Prevention.* Web. 17 April 2010.

Ballard, William A. and Matthew R. Chase. "Nontraditional Recreation Activities: A Catalyst for Quality Physical Education." *JOPERD* 75.3 (March 2004). Print.

Belluck, Pam. "Obesity Rates hit Plateau in U.S., Data Suggest." *New York Times.* 13 January 2010. Web. 15 April 2010.

"Health Consequences." 23 April 2010. *Centers for Disease Control and Prevention.* Web. 26 April 2010.

"Healthy Youth!" 23 April 2010. *Centers for Disease Control and Prevention.* Web. 26 April 2010.

"How much physical activity do children need?" *Centers for Disease Control and Prevention.* 29 March 2010. Web. 17 April 2010.

"Physical Activity and Health: The Benefits of Physical Activity." 29 March 2010. *Division of Nutrition, Physical Activity and Obesity.* 29 March 2010. Web. 17 April 2010.

'Physical Activity in Your Daily Life." *American Heart Association.* 17 April 2010. Web. 17 April 2010.

Summerfield, Liane M. "Promoting Physical Activity and Exercise among Children." *ERIC. Clearinghouse on teaching and Teacher Education.* 20 April 2000. Web. 15 April 2010.

GOT BEEF?

Christina Cocca

Instructor: Kathryn Christolear

Choose a specific social, economic, political, civic, or environmental issue that concerns you and which you wish to explore to discover and justify your own stance on the issue.

When I first got the prompt for this essay, I was sure that I would waver in the direction of issues of capitalism, socialism, democracy, etc. Upon research, I knew my ideas would change yet again. Like every other essay, the writing process always shows me a feeling within myself that I was not yet aware of. After writing a draft that was originally to incorporate beef consumption as just one mere topic of many that I wanted to touch on, I found that I had so much information and could not help but want to share. I decided to focus solely on the problems stemming from the over-consumption of beef, and I feel extremely confident in my choice. After the peer review process was complete, I learned that the information I presented was already affecting people by encouraging them to reassess and reevaluate their personal beef consumption choices. To know that your words reach a person's core is truly worth the research, processes of thought, and efforts contributing to the final product.

The consequences of global warming and environmental damage are so evident that ignorance of our current habits would be irresponsible. Our current culture has recently voiced terms like "green" and the social appeal to "go green" to make the desire to slow down global warming appeal to the masses. "Green" has become a popular term to use in many conversations without full recognition of the seriousness of the situation. The true portrayal of what is really involved in the processes of environmental damages has been skimmed to the mass public numerous times, yet the fact of the matter never seems to fully sink in. The most under-attended issue that has and will become fully necessary for us to examine is our food production, distribution, and intake, with focus on beef and grains. One of the worst habits we are all inadvertently affected by is our over-consumption of beef. The improper utilization of resources required to produce beef as well as the energy required in production pose an undeniable problem to the mass public, thus insinuating the dire need for a reevaluation of our choice on whether to continue high beef consumption.

Evaluation of the effect the government has over the country's execution of environmental-friendly methods is imperative, thus one should consider all aspects of the government's input. Many advertisements are readily available and easily seen via television commercials and print advertisements that encourage people to consume beef and market beef as a primary option for good health, the most recognizable being the "Beef: It's What's For Dinner" slogan. These advertisements are stamped with USDA (United States Department of Agriculture) approval. The funding for the "USDA approved" commercials is supplied by the US government. One might consider where the beef these commercials speak of comes from and how that beef is raised. The beef up for consumption is raised in facilities in which the animals are injected with hormones (which are extremely unhealthy and internally damaging to humans as well as the animals), mistreated, and cruelly and violently slaughtered. These facilities are also funded by the same people in the same government, thus insinuating that a roundabout method of operations is evidently very much active. The USDA has also recently put out a huge campaign in which they specifically mark certain products and food items as "organic" or "organically raised." All that is meant by "organic" is essentially something that has not been chemically altered. In terms of livestock, in order to be considered "organic," the livestock must be reared without the use of any antibiotics or growth hormones and must be fed a healthy diet in which the produce consumed was not genetically modified (United States Department of Agriculture). The same government that funds the USDA's organic stamp is the same government that funds the facilities that bring the need for organic food in the first place. One can conclude that governmental manipulation has infected the public. The monopoly in the government's desire for financial gain from consumers should lead one to feel insulted enough not to participate.

In reality, we might not need as much beef as we think since we are able to get the recommended daily amount of protein from nearly all plant sources. A mere few examples of plant sources that provide adequate amounts of protein are legumes, vegetables, fruits, grains, nuts and seeds. Attention should be paid to soybean, which provides the same amount of protein to the human body as red meat. The human body digests "ninety-two percent of the proteins found in red meats and ninety-one percent of the proteins found in the soybean" (Gertjan). With so many options (virtually every single option that falls under any of the plant source categories), the ability to find protein outside of beef proves to be a situation that yields no difficulty whatsoever since all of the previously named foods are readily available and easily accessible.

The over-consumption of beef is not an economically smart decision that should be made since the long-term future of our resources is in serious jeopardy. For instance, the production of beef for popular consumption requires too many resources and there is not enough land and water for us to continue. Also, the amount of trees that are cut down to make room for grazing land is hardly to be shrugged at when one considers the amount of methane given off by the world's over one billion cows. This amount of methane traps twenty-three times more heat inside the atmosphere than carbon dioxide.

Another unavoidable reason that the consumption of beef is such a huge problem in terms of the environment is the issue of the depletion of food resources. Most of the corn and soy that is grown is used for cattle feed. About two to five times more grain (ten times more in the US) is required to produce the same amount of caloric benefit through livestock than direct consumption of those grains. Seventy percent of American grain production goes to livestock feed (Ajl). Only thirty percent of American grain production is left to be included in foods that provide direct grain intake. The US's over-consumption of beef is also evident by view of the fact that, as a country which yields only five percent of the world's total population, we process (grow and kill) over fifteen percent (about ten billion animals) of the world's total amount of beef processed within one year (Bittman). The factories that treat animals like prey in an assembly line consume heinous amounts of energy, pollute water supplies and generate greenhouse gases. These facilities also require swiftly increasing amounts of soy, grain, and corn for feed which directly leads to the destruction of the Earth's rainforests because of the cutting and burning of rainforests for use as crop and feeding land. In just five months, over twelve-hundred square miles were obliterated from the rainforests (Bittman). Over seventy percent of the Amazon is cleared to make room for cattle-grazing land or to grow soy that will be shipped overseas to feedlots (Kiesel). Greenhouse gas emissions (about twenty-two percent annually) are just one detrimental effect of the depletion of the Amazon. The rainforests are responsible for providing the earth with breathable air, a resource we cannot create ourselves.

With focus on greenhouse gas emissions, only positive results would stem from the reduction of beef consumption. A report by the U.N. Food and Agriculture Organization confirms that "livestock production generates eighteen percent of global GHG (greenhouse gas) emissions," even more greenhouse gases than transportation contributes. The eating of these animals causes forty percent more global warming than all planes, cars, trucks, and other forms of transportation combined. Those emissions include sixty-five percent of human-related nitrous oxide, which has two-hundred ninety-six times the global warming potential of CO_2 (Ajl). The amount of energy required to drive a car and completely light a home for three hours is the same amount of energy needed to produce two pounds of beef (as well as five thousand gallons of water for every two pounds of beef). This statistic does not even include the energy required to run the animal-slaughtering facility, maintain the farm infrastructure, transport the beef to and from the place of export, or the greenhouse gas emissions produced when the forests are wiped out for the animals' grazing land (Ajl). A study last year by the National Institute of Livestock and Grassland Science calculated, "2.2 pounds of beef is responsible for the equivalent amount of carbon dioxide emitted by the average European car every 155 miles, and burns enough energy to light a 100-watt bulb for nearly 20 days" (Bittman). After considering the profuse amounts of energy used to consume beef, an alteration of our decisions to continue seems like such an obvious area to make improvements, especially with the erratic attempts recently made by many to save the dwindling energy resources by switching to electric cars and energy-efficient methods around the home.

The media has not introduced or included an adequate discussion of the topic. This is an issue since the decision on whether one should continue to consume beef or completely cut it out of their diet tends to be a personal choice. One might take offense towards the demand to reconsider one's eating habits, especially since those habits have been formed over the course of a lifetime. However, one must acknowledge the bearing such a specific choice has over the greater social and environmental picture. The decision to cut out beef from the diet is usually from one's passion against the cruelty of animals. The methods in the beef-production facilities by which the animals are raised and slaughtered are extremely unhealthy, cruel, and disturbing. Images that portray the graphic nature of these instances are often mentally-scarring. Given the disturbing nature and the heavy weight of one's moral outlook, the learning of that information and viewing of the images sometimes leads one to the conviction that he or she no longer feels morally right enough to consume beef.

However, moral stance is not the only reason that a person could choose to forgo the inclusion of meat in his or her diet. If the notes on animal cruelty were completely extracted from the mind, and instead one chose to think in the personal, more self-centered way (without consideration for the treatment of animals and only the consideration of one's personal interests), then the limiting (or eliminating altogether) of one's ingestion of beef would still make total and utter sense, since that person is directly affected. As if that one person being undeniably affected is not enough, one could consider how the entire world population is affected by the over-consumption and over-production of beef. The biggest curious quality to the beef debate is the effect that the lowering of beef consumption would actually have on the planet. If the decision to completely cut beef out of our national diet seems too much of a commitment, the reduction of our intake of beef from the average five times a week to just once a week could reduce carbon dioxide emissions by over three-thousand pounds and save well over two-hundred thousand gallons of water per year. With such large numbers, we must consider our earth's carrying capacity, which is the number of people the planet can sustain without irreversibly reducing its capacity to support people in the future. If environmentally abusive habits do not come to a halt, the earth's carrying capacity will inevitably lower. Therefore, the future generations of our children's children will not have enough resources available to assist in their sustainability of life. Essentially, we must concern ourselves with the desire to wisely use resources, which is easily done by the reduction of red meat usage.

The connection between agriculture and climate change is not the only issue we face as a planet, but merely one aspect of the larger issue at hand which is environmental damage. The behaviors we currently partake in (consumption of beef, over-utilization of fuel and grains, etc) are affecting the future generations. If we do not put a halt to irresponsible and selfish actions, our country and earth as a whole is doomed. A world for our children will not exist if these consequences are not fully, thoroughly and seriously examined. Many of the earth's citizens have become blind and selfish, so much so that they do not realize how the actions of today affect the world of tomorrow. If we are set on the improvement of the sustainability of life, we must all consider the benefits of a diet containing noticeably lower amounts of beef with increased amounts of other protein sources (virtually every single fruit and vegetable). In a world that is in serious danger of severe quality depletion, all opportunities for worldwide life-improvement must be taken, and the reduction of beef in the diet is not a huge leap to make when one considers the future generation's environment. The next bite of that cheesy beefy burger will never taste better than having the knowledge of what is done for the world by not biting on the beef bait.

WORKS CITED

Ajl, Max. "Beef: What's Not For Dinner in a Sustainable World." *Solve Climate.* Science First, Inc., 6 Feb. 2009. Web. 6 Nov. 2009.

Bittman, Mark. "Rethinking the Meat-Guzzler." *The New York Times.* The New York Times, 27 Jan. 2008. Web. 9 Nov. 2009.

Gertjan, Schaafsma. "The Protein Digestibility-Corrected Amino Acid Score." *Journal of Nutrition* 130.1865S-1876S (2000): n. pg. JSTOR. Web. 16 Nov. 2009.

Kiesel, Laura. "Why Is the Media Afraid to Tackle Livestock's Role In Climate Change?" *Solve Climate.* Science First, Inc., 6 Feb. 2009. Web. 6 Nov. 2009.

United States Department of Agriculture. "Sustainable Development." *United States Department of Agriculture.* United States Department of Agriculture, 12 Aug. 2009. Web. 5 Dec. 2009.

EDUCATION

"Yes, there is a growing dropout rate in the U.S., but if this is going to be used as evidence to prove the U.S. cannot compete with China and India, then why not show their low dropout rates too?"

—STACEY GAITAN

MAKE THE RHYTHMS HEARD IN PUBLIC EDUCATION
Rosalinda Pozos

Instructor: Andzhela Keshishyan

Consider Steve Lopez's *The Soloist*. In a carefully constructed argumentative essay, discuss the problematic issues of homelessness, mental illness, or music in our society.

As an aspiring high school teacher, I am dismayed at the fact that there is no strong focus in teaching music in public education. Music, rhythms, and sounds are everywhere—they can serve as distractions, concentration, or sole enjoyment. This essay proves that music can help students in various ways and should, therefore, be integrated into their school curriculum.

Music can help heal the soul. Music is life. Many people hear statements like this everywhere, but the seriousness of the statements varies. In *The Soloist*, Steve Lopez elaborates on the fact that music has a strong ability to reform the lives of many people. There are many subjects taught in public schools that expand our knowledge, but unfortunately, music is not one of them. Funding for music education and other fine arts is the first to be removed when a state faces economic troubles and budgeting crisis. Without the education of music in schools, many students' knowledge becomes restricted. It is easy to say that without music, a student misses out on many privileges such as familiarity with musical instruments and sounds which are eminent to life all around us. Because music education has become limited to many people, public education should expand its restricted curriculum to provide students with a wider variety of learning.

In recent years, music education has been at the bottom of the list of things to improve by the government. Jill Leach affirms, "Reduction in state funding have caused the elimination of band and orchestra programs…for the 2009–2010 school year." Unfortunately, the first extra-curricular classes that are eliminated in schools are the fine arts because they seem less important than the academic classes such as math, English and science. This is something that should be addressed in all aspects because it affects students' learning in negative ways. Often times, music and other fine arts in schools make students more interested in continuing their public education. Developing a student's knowledge with music should be the most important part of a student's education; therefore, all efforts should be made to keep music in schools and develop music programs rather than take them away because the state is losing money.

Many students are not given the opportunity to experience for themselves the art of playing a musical instrument. Unless parents deliberately decide to pay for their son or daughter's musical education, they will miss out on an integral part of growing up. Other times, the parents are only able to afford musical education for their son or daughter for a short period of time. In my family, my older sister and I were given lessons for about a year, but stopped because it was too expensive. People who studied music benefit from intellectual advantages in other subjects not related to music. Barbara Occhino states, "The College Board did a study of 10 million students and found that students who take four years of high school arts or more score 98 points higher on the critical reading and math portions of the SAT's." This proves that students with musical knowledge will do better on standardized tests than students who have not had any music classes. Having musical intelligence comes with possible survival skills because it allows for a person to stay alert and manipulates a person's mood. Research has proved that there is "a direct line between music and brain function and improved reading, spatial and verbal skills" (Payne). With this significant proof that music is beneficial, the government should avoid cutting music from the school curriculum.

In a world where the internet and cell phones are taking over children's lives, it is important to teach children valuable lessons about music. If students are not taught about music, they may never understand it. Elizabeth Payne argues, "funding cuts, declining enrollment and a trend toward generalization in teachers means many… students have perhaps never even heard a choir, let alone played an instrument or even learned about music." Because technology makes people impatient, they should be exposed to the calming abilities of music. Music can function as a form of medication or therapy and a means of escaping possible problems that a person may be facing. Eventually, music may become our savior of the madness that technology has caused, but people may not realize it is becoming more and more inaccessible. The powerful sounds and rhythms that songs create help everyone slow down and are more understanding and patient. In her article, Elizabeth Payne briefly mentions that a neurologist wrote a book "about the emotional and therapeutic power of music." Music has become more and more distant to many people because few have taken music classes. Because of this, it will be more difficult to prove to children the importance of music and will move farther away from generation to generation. Even though it is difficult for some people to understand how important music is because it works on a different, more emotional level than math or science, it is nonetheless important and should not be ignored any longer.

Other people are also struggling to find a way to instill music appreciation in students' lives. Jill Leach mentions that "Tustin Public Schools Foundation, Tustin Unified School District and city of Tustin are collaborating on a pilot After-School Music Program for fourth and fifth-graders at weekly after school sessions." Programs such as these will help students learn music and further their knowledge of sounds and rhythms. It is understandable that many people will object to having children learn music but they do not understand the value of introducing music to kids at a young age. Teachers are also finding ways to incorporate music into their classrooms, which can be counterproductive since teachers already have a lot of material to cover and music may end up sounding uninteresting to children. At any level, teachers have thought of ways to incorporate music into classrooms; either by playing different songs in passing period or playing it while the students are working. For example, in one of my high school classes, one of my teachers played classical music while we took tests.

Some people are apathetic about music being in schools and part of the education of children. They may believe that "music, dance, the visual arts, theater and other forms of human expression have little or no place in traditional book learning" (Hardman). Incredibly enough, there is proof that demonstrates that music improves test scores. Others may disagree that "they teach no 'practical' skill or trade and play a small role in the advancement of seemingly more useful subject (Hardman). Music will be able to teach children about different cultures and how each sound determines a person's mood. This powerful piece of art should not be eliminated from schools and public education.

Many people may also disagree with having music in schools and say that teachers are too busy to teach music. Barbara Occhino points out that, "Teachers had a significantly higher degree of innovation in their instruction, were more supportive of students, and had greater interest in their own professional development." This proves that even teachers will benefit from having music taught in their classrooms. To be able to teach music to students, teachers will have to be required to be masterful at the subject. Once they become knowledgeable about music, teachers will benefit from being aesthetically connected to many cultures and see the enjoyment that students feel as they learn about music. Hardman mentions that teachers will be able "to use an integrated curriculum model that teaches children to explore multiple subjects simultaneously" if they participate in the arts and education partnership at the University of Utah. Taking time to implement this, teachers will begin to see the benefits.

As someone who was not able to get enough music knowledge from either playing an instrument or learning about rhythms, it is easy for me to point out the negative effects. For example, there are many students who feel that they were at a disadvantage because they were not given the opportunity to play an instrument. This lack of knowledge leads to the inability to understand the kinds of instruments that are used in songs. Knowing the impact of not teaching children music develops the notion that everyone needs to help the students and create programs so that they will not miss out on a big part of their lives.

Even though many states are suffering from lack of funding, cutting schools' fine arts and music programs will not ameliorate the economic crisis. The government needs to understand that even though many students will not make a career in music, it will benefit them in the future. As Kathy Bushouse points out, "Four schools in the same zone would share a media specialist along with an art, music and physical education teacher." It is unfair that students would have to suffer the disadvantages of not having their own music teacher and to have to share because the government is unable to make correct choices about state budgets. Music should become part of the public education curriculum and will motivate students to want to learn more about the arts.

Unfortunately, not everyone is interested in the arts and music. Charles Clark mentions, "With the arts of major importance to fewer than a third of all Americans, some observers worry that the efforts of arts boosters could be easily thwarted in this era of budget deficits and shrinking roles for government." This type of thinking is not beneficial to all of the people who struggle to get music education to be mandatory in public schools. Although making people realize that music is an integral part of our education is difficult, it can be accomplished through hard work and determination. Once people begin to understand the importance of having music as a part in music education, it will be easier to integrate it into the school system.

To avoid fine art cuts in public education, the government needs to understand that music is vital for students. Despite the fact that students with a musical background will be more intelligent, the government should realize that music helps students emotionally as well. Music is a powerful art that should not be restricted to those who are able to afford it, but rather available for everyone to benefit from. When everyone begins to learn about music, they will appreciate it and be able to find the many rhythms that compose their lives such as the footsteps of someone walking or the sound of leaves rustling in the trees. Music education should not be left as a mere afterthought in school curriculum but rather one of the first things to improve in the United States.

Works Cited

Bushouse, Kathy. "Broward Schools to Consider Cuts to Arts, Music, Physical Education Classes: Elementary Programs Face Big Changes Next Year." *ProQuest.* 9 Mar. 2010. Web. 30 Mar. 2010.

Clark, Charles S. "Arts Funding." *CQ Researcher.* 21 Oct. 1994. Web. 30 Mar. 2010.

Hardman, Michael L. Raymond Tymas-Jones "U. to Lead the Way in Arts Education." *Deseret News.* 2 Mar. 2008. *ProQuest.* Web. 30 Mar. 2010.

Leach, Jill. "Partnership Is 'music to Their Ears'" *Orange County Register.* 27 Aug. 2009. *ProQuest.* Web. 30 Mar. 2010.

Occhino, Barbara. "Don't Cut the Arts in Our Schools." *Advocate.* 20 Mar. 2009. *ProQuest.* Web. 30 Mar. 2010.

Payne, Elizabeth. "The Sound of Music." *The Ottawa Citizen.* 6 May 2008. *ProQuest.* Web. 30 Mar. 2010.

SAT: VITAL OR UNNECESSARY?

Zain Shammas

Instructor: Lynne Miller

Determine a civic argument, an argument dealing with government, people, society, and community.

The inspiration behind "SAT: Vital or Unnecessary?" was from a close friend who was not accepted into a university seemingly due to his average SAT scores. He was an excellent student with a 3.7 GPA but had average SAT scores which led the University to deny acceptance. I also experienced this problem with my own SAT scores, and felt inspired to truly ask readers if they think a student's collegiate life should be based so much upon a single standardized test.

One of the most important factors of the college application process is the SAT Reasoning Test, an aptitude test that is given to students in order to determine their overall knowledge of subjects. Most well established colleges require average to above average scores on the SAT for admission into their schools. The SAT is part of the application process, which also includes a student's overall GPA, letters of recommendation, a report of extracurricular activities, and a completed information form, which may include an essay or two, depending on the college's preference. Although it is truly unknown how influential a student's SAT score is towards his acceptance, it is believed that, if it comes down to the wire, colleges will select a student with a higher score than a student with a lower score, despite the differences between them. This idea leaves the majority of students wondering if the SAT scores are in fact fair and are actually reflective of their overall knowledge. Due to the uncertainty of just how well the SAT scores truly reflect a student's knowledge in relation to how important they are in the college admission process, it would be more beneficial to the students if the SAT were abolished from the process.

The SAT Reasoning Test is a test that is required by most colleges for admission and includes three different sections, including a math section, a critical reading section, and a writing section, which requires a brief essay to demonstrate the student's writing skills. Each section contains a possible 800 points and a minimum of 200 points, meaning that the median would be about 1500 points overall, or 500 points for each section. The test is given at many schools across the country, and is also available overseas, and the run time is around four hours (Smith). The ACT is another test that can either act as a substitute for the SAT or an additional reference for students to test their knowledge and prove to universities that they are worthy of admission. Slightly different, and to some more challenging, the ACT consists of an English section, which includes a freshman college English section, along with reading comprehension, and a challenging math section, which includes trigonometry. There is also a writing section to be done in the final 30 minutes of the test, which is similar to the SAT, but is optional on the ACT. The main differences between the two tests are that the ACT also has a science section, students are not penalized for wrong answers, and it is graded on a different scale than the SAT (Ellis-Christensen). The purpose of the two tests is to determine the overall knowledge of the student and how they rank against the other applicants in their class. The question is: how well do these tests indicate that information and is it fair to base acceptance on those scores alone?

One of the factors that make the SAT detrimental to students is the fact that it does not accurately reflect a student's knowledge all the time. The aptitude test is developed to indicate a student's overall knowledge by asking both average and challenging questions about the different subjects, but there seems to be no consistency. There are SAT guides, classes, and tutorials on how to "beat the SAT" or for students to simply be prepared. These tools are created to help ease students' minds and benefit them when taking the test. With all of these different study options, one has to wonder if the test is a true aptitude test after all. Wouldn't an aptitude test require no prior studying in order to distinguish a student's level of intellect, rather than that student taking classes to get ahead of the others? If an average student shelled out the money for books and classes to help them on the SAT got a higher score than a straight-A student, who had an off-morning and did not perform as well, would that be fair? These are the questions that researchers are wondering when realizing just how important universities think these scores are, when in fact, they are not even consistent with a student's knowledge.

In "The Russian Roulette of SAT Scores," Chris Teare mentions how his child was not allowed admission into an impressive university due to this subpar SAT score, despite his amazing track record, including straight A's and a long list of extracurricular activities to his name (Teare 27). He goes on to question if the schools should continue to consider the SAT more important than a student's GPA when a student has four years to create a solid GPA and four hours to manage a good SAT score. Although some may say that the SAT is based more on overall intellect, there is no argument that a student's overall work ethic, mixed in with their ability to get consistent grades, for example, a strong GPA, is more impressive than cramming for the SAT and managing to walk away with an above average score.

Along with not being a credible reflection of a student's knowledge, the SAT test is also viewed by some as unnecessary because it is essentially meaningless. According to Leonard Mlodinow, "the College Board claims that the predictions created by the SAT scores are equal to, if not less accurate, than a student's high school GPA." With the results of this study in mind, it is clear that the SATs do not adequately represent a student's knowledge in any different way than their regular grades on their high school transcripts. Some may argue that the SATs are beneficial for those who did not take school seriously, earned low grades, and thus the test becomes their only chance to do well and redeem themselves. This theory disapproves the idea that the SAT is truly important for students to take because it shows that the overall GPA a student achieves basically reflects the same information of a student's knowledge that a standardized test would.

The controversy against the SAT is found in many different schools all across the country, but there hasn't been much action against it in the form of abolishing the test completely, but there have been many surveys and even petitions that have all dealt with the existence and influence of the test. Although not many schools have acted out, there are some examples, such as American University in Washington D.C., that have dropped the SAT and ACT requirement for their early-decision applicants. This move was more of an incentive to attract students than to please them, but it still managed to incorporate the student's needs into the plan. In the article, "American U. Drops SAT and ACT Requirements for Early-Decision Applicants," the author explains that the dropping of the tests will be part of a one-year program to test how many students would actually decline sending their SAT scores, versus the number of students that would opt to include them in their transcripts. The other part of the program is to see how it affects the instructors who review the applications and judge who is allowed acceptance (Ashburn). The test is still ongoing but officials expect it to highly increase incentive of incoming students and if the plan works, they will stick to the optional test.

Does this mean that the SAT and ACT are really not important to universities and should be abolished? Well, not exactly, but it proves the point that the tests do not consistently show the absolute knowledge that a student has, therefore making it unfair for acceptance to be judged on those scores. Although it can be argued that a lot of other factors come into play during admission to a university and that an SAT score is only used as an extra resource, there are always the scenarios where the scores would be the most important statistic on the application. For example, if there was one spot open at a university, and the decision was between two average students, it is more than likely that the student with the higher SAT score would be admitted. That may seem fair to some, but the fact that a student's acceptance is based on a four hour test is not fair to all students. With more research being done on how the SATs influence a student's acceptance, more universities will most likely join American U. in either not basing their acceptance solely on those scores, leaving the test as an option for students, or simply abolishing it from their admissions process.

Works Cited

Ashburn, Elyse. "American U. Drops SAT and ACT Requirements for Early-Decision Applicants." *Chronicles of Higher Education.* 56 2 (2009): A43. EBSCO. Web. 20 Nov. 2009.

Ellis-Christensen, Tricia. "What is Act Testing?" *Wisegeek.com.* Web. 20 Nov. 2009.

Mlodinow, Leonard. "The SAT: An Essay in Uncertainty." *Chronicle of Higher Education.* 54. 45 (2009): A30. *Academic Search Elite.* Web. 19 Nov. 2009.

Smith, S.E. "What is the SAT?" *Wisegeek.com* Web. 20 November. 2009.

Teare, Chris. "The Russian Roulette of SAT Scores." *The Chronicle of Higher Education.* 55. 36 (2009): 27. *LexisNexis Academic.* Web. 19 Nov. 2009.

U.S. EDUCATION
Stacey E. Gaitan

Instructor: Kimberly Wells

To what extent is the education system in the United States preparing its citizens to be successful in a global economy?

The inspiration for this essay came from the documentary Two Million Minutes, *produced and created by Robert A. Compton. The documentary focuses on the idea that the U.S. is falling behind China and India as far as competitiveness in the global market. As I began writing this essay I wanted to prove that the U.S. is still competing in the global market and bring light to the vast opportunities students have due to our diverse curriculum. At first this essay became very overwhelming because of the great amount of research it required and after my first draft I was unsure of whether or not I would be able to make my position clear. As I reviewed my final draft, however, I could happily say that I defended my position well and hopefully will encourage discussion about this topic.*

The U.S. education system is still capable of producing successful and competitive individuals to uphold the country's reputation in the global market. Although it is true that countries like China and India are making great advances in math and science and are becoming much more competitive than before, the U.S. is still a strong competitor. U.S. Education is more well-rounded; while subjects like math and science are important, so are extracurricular activities such as sports and art. There are many opportunities to create a successful career being the next Lil Wayne of music or Alex Rodrigez of baseball. However, in countries such as China and India, the opportunity to become a successful athlete, actor, or artist are not as accepted by their societies' standards. The U.S. education system carries a more diverse curriculum that allows its student to branch out and excel in many areas, yet it still has the ability to produce quality engineers and mathematicians. Therefore, the U.S. may be falling behind in the number of representatives it has in science and math compared to China and India, but the opportunities given to the many entrepreneurs and innovative minds of this country ensure that the U.S. will continue to compete in the global economy.

The diverse curriculum implemented in the U.S. education system allows for its students to be innovative in fields ranging from math and science to music and sports, but seeming lack of strict focus on academics leads some to doubt its ability to compete in the global economy. This topic is brought up in the documentary *Two Million Minutes* produced and created by Robert A. Compton. In it, one follows the everyday life of two U.S., two Chinese, and two Indian high school students. The documentary shows Rohit Srindhara, one of the Indian students, commenting, "it's academics or nothing else." This shows the mentality of students in India where academics are for the most part the only choice if one wants to be successful. Unfortunately, they do not share the same opportunities provided in the U.S. For instance, according to the *New York Daily News*, former Super Bowl champion and current Giants quarterback, Eli Manning, recently signed a $97.5 million, six year contract extension. While American football may not be played in

China or India, it is this type of success in athletics that is as widely promoted in either country as it is here. In the documentary, one can also see Rohit Srindhara singing in a group with his friends as a hobby. Music is another career outlet that has become very popular and is well supported in the U.S. It has given birth to many great entrepreneurs, such as Russell Simmons. He is the founder and former president of Def. Jam Records. Sean "Diddy" Combs is another example of an artist turned businessman. Many may not see how this helps the U.S. compete globally, but it is the ability students have to choose a career in something they are passionate about that gives them the drive to be innovative in whatever field they choose. This inevitably leads to persistence and success that will help this country continue growing.

The fear that the U.S. has fallen behind and can no longer compete with China and India is not credible because these statements come from narrowly focused statistics. Danny Vaughn, a professor of Geosciences, writes in his article for *Examiner.com* "China now produces eight times more scientists and engineers, while India graduates three times as many as the United States." Statistics like this one are seen throughout Compton's documentary; one cannot help but feel as though there is a bias in this opinion. According to a story done by ABC News, The National Association of Secondary School Principals critiqued the documentary for "…Providing statistics about drop out rates in the United States, but never mentions similar statistics from China or India." Yes, there is a growing dropout rate in the U.S., but if this is going to be used as evidence to prove the U.S. cannot compete with China and India, then why not show their low dropout rates too? One-sided evidence, such as this, causes skepticism of the facts presented. One cannot accept an opinion as fact without having all the information. For instance, a news story done for *China Daily* in 2006 stated that "According to Mu Zhen, an official with the provincial education department, there are about 40,000 pupils who have dropped out of school in Shaanxi." As for India, Vineeta Pandey wrote "…each year about 48% of students are "washed out" of the education system as they reach the secondary level …India's gross enrolment rate (GER) at the secondary level is 40%…" These statistics are never mentioned in articles or videos promoting China and India's educational superiority. When one compares equal evidence from all sides, it is evident that the globalization race is still ongoing and that the U.S. continues to be a strong competitor.

In competition, people tend to show their best assets, leaving their flaws hidden; countries striving to be global leaders are no different. The National Association of Secondary School Principals states "the film focuses exclusively on math, science and engineering, but doesn't consider excellence in other subjects…"about the *Two Million Minutes* documentary in a story done by ABC News. Pointing out the constricted perspective displayed throughout most of the film, which is similar to the many articles and stories being written about the U.S.'s shortcomings in comparison to China and India. It may not be lying when one hides their weaknesses, but there is an obvious bias when one only presents its strengths. Young Zhao, a Michigan State University professor, points out, "I think tests are biased to reflect the talents that other cultures emphasize more." The U.S. could do the same by bringing out statistics that only represent their strong suits. Professor Zhao goes on to add, "we have many more possible outlets for talents, and that's actually much more important." A fact many people lose sight of when considering the arguments presented by the competition. The U.S. has not lost this race; it is simply pacing itself and taking time to strategize, taking into consideration all the possibilities.

The United States has held a global leadership position for a long time and it has maintained this position by staying true to the roots of this country, so those who believe it is a good idea to adapt the educational methods of other countries are wrong. One cannot successfully compete if one is too busy trying to imitate the competition. As Professor Zhao has said, "Americans should be more American—not more Chinese or Japanese or Singaporean – in our education." One must stand by their methods, which have proven to be effective before. Professor Zhao adds that he believes the key to Americans succeeding in the future is "the ability to manage across different cultures." The U.S. should not try to adapt China and India's Educational system or copy their narrowly focused standards. Instead, the U.S. should realize that our educational system has the liberty of being more diverse due to the opportunities it has made available to its students—opportunities that have been created by the great creative and innovative minds developed by their education system. The U.S. must remain true to itself in order to successfully compete globally.

It is possible that in the fields of math and science, the U.S. has been surpassed by China and India, but it is not true that the U.S. is no longer a global competitor. The U.S. is still competing. Those who argue otherwise have merely been presenting evidence to support their claims, spreading biased statistics. The U.S. has always been recognized by other countries for its creativity and innovative ideas that stem from the diverse curriculum it implements. It will always be a competitor in the global market because of the foundation of diversity it stands on and the vast amount of opportunities it provides for its students to be successful.

Works Cited

2 Million Minutes. Dir. Robert A. Compton. Broken Pencil Productions, 2007. DVD.

"Film: U.S. Students Can't Compete in High-Tech World." *ABC News.* 20 Feb. 2008. Web. 12 Oct. 2009.

Khadraoo, Stacy T. "World's schools teach U.S. a lesson." *Csumonitor.com.* 14 Nov. 2007. Web. 12 Oct. 2009.

Pandey, Vineeta. "Primary crisis is in secondary schools." *Dnaindia.com.* 7 Oct. 2009. Web. 19 Oct. 2009.

"Project to Help Rural Kids Go Back to School." *China Daily.* 24 Aug. 2006. Web. 19 Oct. 2009.

Vacchiano, Ralph. "Giants QB Eli Manning signs $97.5 million, six year contract extension." *New York Daily News.* 14 Aug. 2009. Web. 13 Oct. 2009

Vaughn, Danny. "College Bound 101: Does the United States have the most progressive educational system in the world?" *Examiner.com.* 17 Aug. 2009. Web. 12 Oct. 2009.

MODERN TECHNOLOGY AND MEDIA

"The media has shortcomings, but this is showbiz. The show must go on. It is not just up to them, but also up to us to keep us from fearing the boogey man."

—GREGORY CARLSON

THE COST OF HIGH RATINGS
Gregory Carlson

Instructor: Casey Chainee

Analyze and evaluate the following question: To what extent does racism exist in the United States today?

I thought about writing this article after a lecture that my professor had given in my Intro to Central American Studies 100 class (CAS 100) about the previous night's reading. It was called "Breaking the Vicious Cycle: Responding to Central American Youth Gang Violence" by Lainie Reisman. The article talked about how news coverage of gang violence in El Salvador actually fed a cycle of gang violence and poverty. I wanted to explore how similar types of cycles might exist in America and try to link it to the topic of racism.

The media holds an incredible power. It is the power of having millions of people believe every word they say and then using those words to form an opinion. Many times this power is used to feed the people of America valuable and worthwhile knowledge that helps people make positive contributions to society. Ideally, it is purely entertaining and has no effect beyond the emotions that it was intended to cause, but there are times when this power is used to instill fear and misinformation in people. These are times when people have been frightened into relinquishing their rights for the notion of security. The media's influence over public perception has led to the passage of government policies such as the Terrorist Prevention Act, as well as the Illegal Immigrant policy in California that support racism.

One of the most recent threats to national security is terrorism. On September 11, 2001, the World Trade Center was struck by two hijacked commercial airliners. The buildings collapsed, killing thousands of innocent people. It was a dark day in America's history, and we will forever mourn those who died in that tragic incident. For many years afterwards, America was paralyzed by the fear of another attack; however, a fear that carries on for this long cannot be perpetuated by a single event. Beyond the initial shock of being unexpectedly attacked on American soil, news outlets constantly gave reports about the aftermath of the event. The press was and, in many ways, still is inundated with news related to the events of 9/11.

Reports like the *New York Times* coverage of President Obama's speech on National Security presented on May 21st 2009 imply, through the report's existence, that we are still in danger and need security. In a November 20, 2009 publication of the *New York Times* titled, "U.S. Fears Iraqis Will Not Keep Up Rebuilt Projects," the author shows concern about the social stability of Iraq, and a quote by former Vice President Dick Cheney in 2004 further promotes the idea of another terrorist attack: "They have attacked our nation and they wish to do us further harm. But with the leadership of this president and the resilience of the American people, we will meet the challenges of our time" (Lyman). The list goes on. This constant barrage of frightening scenarios must have some lasting effect on the people of America because the Intelligence Reform and Terrorist Prevention Act of 2004 was passed as a law, a full three years after the event. This law proposed security methods for preventing possible terrorists from attacking, or even entering the country again. It reestablished a "no-fly" list that would deny those on the list passage onto airlines in or to America. It also employed a pre-screening service that would screen all passengers on flights to America for legal passport and selective interrogation for possible terrorist action. These measures can and have been used to target ethnic groups such as Muslims of Middle Eastern decent whom Americans unjustly associate with terrorists. The media supports these means of security, if not directly, then through its control of public perception and its exploitation of racial stereotypes. Articles like the ones listed above only feed the fear caused by 9/11 and lead Americans to support a government practice that is discriminatory.

Another racist policy spurred by the media is illegal immigration. The reason it is such a debated issue is because the media portrays illegal immigrants as crooks and gang bangers who come to America to kill people and take all of the unskilled jobs. The media says that illegal immigrants raise health insurance rates and hurt the economy. While some of these statements are fundamentally true, they fail to address the root of the problem. For example, an article published in the *LA Times* titled "Illegal Immigrants Wiring Money Have an Amigo: The Feds," author Molly Hennessy-Fisk addresses how illegal immigrant workers hurt the economy by sending their earnings to relatives in Mexico or Honduras, but she fails to discuss why so many illegal immigrants feel the need to send their money home. From this view of illegal immigrants, debates continue to flare up in California. These confrontations have led to immigrant policies in California such as "Zero Tolerance Policing," a policy exercised by police that involves inflicting the maximum punishment possible for petty crimes. This practice is more commonly enforced against Latino people and more than often leads to deportation; that is because Latino people are often portrayed in the media as drug dealers and gang members. This stereotyping has led to fear and misunderstanding in California over illegal immigrants and gangs that actually perpetuate their situation.

In a case study conducted by Lainie Reisman of the illegal immigrant policy between California and the Central American countries like Mexico, El Salvador, and Honduras, she suggests in her article of the study titled "Breaking the Vicious Cycle: Responding to Central American Youth Gang Violence," that the media campaigning against gangs actually feeds a cycle that is a result of California's intense immigrant policy and Central America's improvised state (Reisman). Reisman's cycle goes as such: media campaigning leads to more investment in security which means less investment in public services. This creates more incentive to join gangs, which leads to more gang violence, which leads to more investment in security. The reason that the media campaigning is more likely to promote racist policy is the fact that the media fails to shed light on the individual. They never tried to help us understand the gang member, but instead worked to make us fear the gang. This has led to the racial profiling of young Latino/Central American men as gang members. These people cannot stand at street corners with their friends without taking the risk of being interrogated by the police. If the media takes more time to help us understand the individual gang member or illegal immigrant, then they will likely find a much different story of someone who was out of options and forced to take a dangerous path. Instead, their argument only involves the faceless generalizations. These kinds of impersonal broadcasts do not give the whole story and have molded the public perception to be one of dislike and discrimination of illegal immigrants and gang members.

Some may blame the government for invoking such measures against terrorism and illegal immigration. It is true that many of the news reports previously mentioned in this article are of government figures promoting limited views. The government is the one enforcing biased policies after all. The problem with this idea is that this is a sovereign society, which means that the power is in the people. It is true that the government asks us to sign these bills, but we are the ones who signed it. We did it because we were afraid. We were afraid because the things that we saw and heard gave us reason to be afraid. Most of the things we see and hear about the world are on a television or computer screen. While the government officials were talking, the media was filming. The two go hand in hand when altering public perception, but while the government needs the media to influence public opinion, the media is not as bound to the government in doing so.

But we, the people of America, have a right to see and hear the things that the media broadcasts to us. They are just doing their jobs. This is a very common argument for the media. One example of the media using the argument of 'we are just doing our jobs' is in an *America's Intelligence Wire* article titled "The Buffalo News, N.Y., Alan Pergament column: In covering Palin, media is just doing its job" by Alan Pergament. In the article, Pergament defends the media from being called "left wing" for their coverage of Sarah Palin. Another one is in the *Asia Africa Intelligence Wire* article titled "The media is just doing its job with Tung's foibles" where they are being accused of assaulting the government with their articles. Media outlets are just giving us what we expect of them. They have no intention of promoting racist political policy. The issue is that they have a choice. There is a lot of news out there. The media has the option of choosing between writing about a gang related shooting, the economic consequences of illegal immigrants, or possible plans for another terrorist attack. They also have the choice of telling us about why these people are joining gangs, what hardships these immigrants are facing, or how the people of Iraq are dealing with change. It is the Media's duty to give us the whole story, but by not doing so, they have created an unjustified public opinion of many things that have led to the passage of implicitly discriminatory laws.

It may seem grim, but it is not as bad as it seems. There are just as many forms of media that promote a positive image of people and attempt to combat public hysteria. This is the other side of the coin: where media can be used as a source of discrimination and paranoia, it can also be used to promote understanding. There are broadcasts that have shed light on the individual gang member as well as the probability of a second 9/11. These are the ones that understand the incredible power that they hold. It is the duty of the media to give the whole story. In addition, it is the duty of the recipient to seek out the whole story. While it is true that in many situations the media fails to do their duty, it is still up to the recipients to save themselves from ignorance, learn more about the issues, and "question [their] beliefs" (Chainee). Ask yourself who might be affected by the implementation of this bill. It just might be you. Ask yourself why these people are making the perilous journey to America in the first place. The answer just might surprise you. Good media is out there. It just takes some searching.

The media can be a dangerous thing. It has the power both to create and to destroy. It can create understanding about the issue at hand by providing fair and unbiased knowledge with which a proper opinion can be formulated. It can destroy understanding too. A biased report will give partial truths and sometimes misinformation that leads to an unjust opinion. These fabricated opinions can be dangerous because they can lead to fear among the masses. Those who fear are often willing to sacrifice their freedoms for projected security, and the consequences have often been the implication of discriminatory practices in the government, practices such as a "No Fly" list which has been used to harass ethnic groups such as Muslims. It has also led to "Zero Tolerance Policing," which has resulted in the separation of young Hispanic teenagers from their families to be sent to a place that they may have only spent their very early childhood in and who do not speak Spanish. More than not, the repercussions of the media cannot be predicted. It was never the media's intention to contribute to governmental racism the way they have done. Ultimately, it was the failure to do something that led to their mistake. It was the failure to get the entire story. It was the failure to consider the implications. It was the failure to consider the individual. The media has shortcomings, but this is showbiz. The show must go on. It is not just up to them, but also up to us to keep us from fearing the boogey man.

Works Cited

Chainee, Casey. California State University, Northridge. Jerome Richfield, room 247. 16 November 2009. Lecture.

Florence, Justin. "Making the No Fly List Fly: A Due Process Model for Terrorist Watchlists." *Yale Law Journal* 115.8 (2006): 2148–2182. *General OneFile*. Web. 23 November 2009.

Hennessy-Fiske, Molly. "Illegal Immigrants Wiring Money have an Amigo: The Feds." *LAtimes.com*. Los Angeles Times. 26 February 2007. Web. 23 November 2009.

Lyman, Rick. "The Republicans: The Convention in New York—The Vice President; Cheney Tries to Stir Memories of Bush in Days After 9/11." *NYtimes.com*. New York Times. 30 August 2004. Web. 23 November 2009.

Pergament, Alen. "The Buffalo News, N.Y., Alan Pergament column: in Covering Palin, Media is just doing its job." *America's Intelligence Wire*. 5 September 2008. *General OneFile*. Web. 24 November 2009.

Reisman, Lainie. "Breaking the Vicious Cycle: Responding to Central American Youth Gang Violence." *Introduction to Central American Studies*. Eds. Beatriz Cortez and Douglas Carranza Mena. Dubuque, Iowa. Kendall/Hunt Publishing Company, 2008. 266–72. Print.

"The Media is just doing its job with Tung's Foibles. *Asia Africa Intelligence Wire* 30 December 2004. *General OneFile*. Web. 24 November 2009.

Williams, Timothy. "U.S. Fears Iraqis Will Not Keep up Rebuilt Projects." *NYtimes.com*. New York Times. 20 November 2009. Web. 23 November 2009.

DO YOU FEEL VIOLENT AFTER PLAYING PONG?

Garrick Raigosa

Instructor: Desi Bradley

Writer's Choice Argument

Being an avid video game follower, I already knew much about the topic of violent video games. Many times, I have heard games blamed for people acting violently and every time, I would feel enraged by it. People are ignorant that video games are nothing more than a fun pastime and do not turn you into violent killers. I saw this essay as a chance to finally speak about what I feel in a more professional means. The Oviatt Library online search databases allowed me to cite lab experiments verifying my arguments. With the aid of scientific proof, writing this essay became engaging and easy.

The video game industry is currently being used as the scapegoat for violence in society. If a teenage boy happens to show any signs of aggression or violence, no matter how extreme or minimal, before checking his family life, school life, or relationships, the question "what games was he playing" is asked. Video games can allow for the player to do practically anything if the game gives the option and that includes most forms of violence. Because of this, video games are placed under the watchful eyes of politicians, parent watch groups, and the media. These groups claim that violent video games cause an increase in aggression in the people playing them. Since 1996, steps have been made to get video games banned or at the very least, highly restricted. Media outlets such as Fox News, have claimed video games have taken things too far. They said, "[if] You bring a violent game into a house with an 8-year-old, [there is] nothing to stop that kid from playing it and becoming a terrorist...on a video game," in regards to a video game known as *Call of Duty: Modern Warfare 2* (Ashcraft). To claim that a game about war can turn a child into a terrorist is not only absurd, but also misleading. Video games do not deserve this discrimination and censorship because no true link between aggression and video games has been found. Furthermore, the history of other mediums shows that this is a struggle that needs to be experienced. There is already a prevention system in place to stop anyone who should not be playing these games.

The largest claim people make against video games is that playing violent video games makes people more aggressive. For anyone who has never actually played a modern game or at least understands them, this theory makes sense. In a study to determine what people think of the negative effects of video games, James D. Ivory and Sriram Kalyanaraman explained their results: "Our findings pertaining to the effects of person abstraction on perceived negative media effects [violent video game effects] are consistent with previous findings indicating that abstraction (i.e., vagueness) is a component of the social distance construct that influences people's perceptions of negative media effects [aggression] on others" (Ivory and Kalyanaraman). According to this research, people only believe video games can have negative effects because their understandings of games are vague. Video games like the popular series *Grand Theft Auto* allow the player to not only hijack a car and pick up a prostitute, but it then allows them to run them over with said car and get their money back after everything is said and done. Now it would seem that it would take a violent person to actually do that violent stuff. However, that's not really the truth. The last installment in the *Grand Theft Auto* series has sold 13 million copies as of March, 2009. Following the current opinion on video games, the number of copies that the *Grand Theft Auto* series sold for imply that there are that many violent people around and that number just seems impossible. That is a lot of people who are considered violent. It is arguable to say that these violent games actually prevent people from doing violent things because they can get it out of their system in the game rather than in real life. A violent video game becomes no different than a virtual punching bag which helps get out aggression. To say that the people who are playing this violent game are violent themselves is extremely ignorant. There have been many experiments made in hopes of finding an answer to this problem. Unfortunately, results have varied from experiment to experiment.

For instance, a study by the American Psychological Association concluded that playing violent video games caused higher aggression and retaliatory thoughts in people than those who play non-violent games. They got these results by allowing the person who lost in the violent game to get revenge against their opponent by using a "noise blast." By measuring the amount the loser would use the blast and for how long, they made their conclusion. One of the doctors on the study concluded by saying:

> Violent video games provide a forum for learning and practicing aggressive solutions to conflict situations. In the short run, playing a violent video game appears to affect aggression by priming aggressive thoughts. Longer-term effects are likely to be longer lasting as well, as the player learns and practices new aggression-related scripts that can become more and more accessible for use when real-life conflict situations arise. ("Violent Video Games Can Increase Aggression")

The increase in "aggressive thoughts" is not too surprising. If someone is exposed to violent video games in a lab designed to measure violence, then they are more prone to think aggressively. Now those thoughts do sound worrisome; however, most people are wise enough to differentiate thoughts from actions. For this lab to be valid, a study would need to be made to determine the transfer rate between these thoughts and actual actions. Perhaps those studies are not being made because the numbers would be quite low and would not conform to the lab's bias. But even after that follow-up study, what about the winner of the game? Why is that person not studied? Couldn't winning a game offer the same relaxing experience as a basketball player winning a big match? The study's bias to show a negative outcome in this situation becomes increasingly obvious once other non-negative studies are viewed.

A similar study conducted by Christopher J. Ferguson showed completely different results. His analysis "indicates that the extant literature on video game violence effects conducted during the "third" era of video games has not provided compelling support to indicate either a correlational or causal relationship between violent game play and actual aggressive behavior" (Ferguson). There was no link found between aggressive behavior and violent games. In another study by Tobias Greitemeyer and Silvia Osswald, video games were actually found to reduce aggression. They conclude that "two experiments lend credence to our hypothesis that playing prosocial video games decreases aggressive responses. More specifically, playing a prosocial video game reduced the expectation that other people respond with aggressive behavior, thoughts, and feelings (Experiment 1) and decreased the accessibility of antisocial thoughts (Experiment 2)" (Greitemeyer and Osswald). Although those prosocial games were not violent, it only lends credence that games should be taken more seriously as a medium.

Long before video games became popular, all forms of entertainment had to go through the same struggle of being accused of causing violence. Television was regarded as another medium through which children could be exposed to violence. Music was said to make kids violent by letting them listen to violent songs. Now video games are accused of making kids violent. Both video games and music were the topics of Congressional hearings in the past. In these hearings, the goal was to determine the nation's right to censor each medium under the claim that the population can become increasingly violent from their influence. Music and Video Games were taken to Congress by the Parental Music Resource Center and Senators Joe Lieberman and Herb Kohl respectively (Kohler). Instead of the outright banning of the mediums, a group or system was set in place to restrict each medium from getting in the hands of those deemed unfit. In the case of video games, the Entertainment Software Ratings Board was founded, which will be discussed later. In music's case, the Parental Advisory warning was set up for content deemed worthy of it. Music is no longer seen in the negative light that it once was because of these regulations and this leads many to believe the same will happen with video games eventually. It's a highly likely assumption this will happen when looking at the history of music and television.

When the day comes that video games are finally taken seriously as a medium and a hobby, and finally accepted by society, parents around the world will still be concerned that their kids may become aggressive from these violent games. Based on the notion that children are easily influenced, these concerns are understandable. The results from a study of children from 11 to 15 years old by the Swinburne University of Technology, showed that most of the children were found to be unaffected by the games with the only exclusion being those that are already predisposed to aggression.. Swinburne's Professor Devilly says, "You've got to basically read your own kid. If you have a quite hyper kid, they will calm down after playing a bit, but for the rest of kids, the vast majority, it makes no difference at all in their general aggression rate" ("Most kids 'unaffected'"). However, even with this information, there will never be a way to stop parents from being concerned that their children could become violent after seeing the gory visuals of violent games. But there is already a system in place that should put those worries to rest; it's called the ESRB.

The Entertainment Software Ratings Board is an independently regulated ratings system put in place by the video game industry. The ESRB determines a letter rating for each game placed on the market according to specific guidelines on a game's content. The ratings range from EC for Early Childhood to AO for adults only. Although most consumers will find that the ratings E for everyone, T for teen (13 and older), and M for mature (17 and older) are the most common. From a state to state basis, laws have been erected that force all stores to adhere to these ratings. What that means is that a twelve year old child cannot go to his local game store to buy an M rated game without a consenting adult. A store will be fined by the government if they are not following this law. But some outspoken watch groups may claim this isn't an effective prevention system because there is no one to enforce it. However, in an article by the Federal Trade Commission, it was found that kids trying to buy M rated games by themselves are turned away an overwhelming 80% of the time and GameStop, the nation's largest video game focused retailer has a 94% turn away rate ("Undercover Shoppers"). But beyond this system should be the best system: the parents. Despite warnings from the ESRB regarding the content of certain games; ultimately, it is the parents' choice to decide. The parents can still buy whatever game they want for their child no matter how violent. It is the parents' duty to stay informed and be aware of what their children should and should not play, and if they decide to let their child play a violent game, it is their responsibility to teach their child the difference between reality and the game.

Video games are still seen as children's toys. Because of this, politicians and watch groups are trying to do the parenting for the nation by censoring video games in fear that a violent video game will cause another school shooting, no matter how much evidence disproves the links between aggression and games. The video game industry feels the effects of this fear and has put the ESRB in place. The only thing people should be concerned about is children's access to violent games. However, children have little chance of getting a mature game themselves. In a survey by media research firm Harrison Group and video game publisher Activision, 84% of the parents interviewed were "very familiar" with the ESRB ratings system ("Parents recognize"). Through progress like this, video games will finally be free of any blame cast on it and gamers everywhere can go back to enjoying their games rather than worrying if they're being called violent for doing so.

Work Cited

Ashcraft, Brian. "Modern Warfare 2 on Fox & Friends." *Kotaku*. 11 Nov. 2009. Web. 19 Nov. 2009.

Ferguson, Christopher J. "Aggression and Violent Behavior : Evidence for publication bias in video game violence effects literature: A meta-analytic review." *ScienceDirect*. 3 Feb. 2007. Web. 08 Nov. 2009.

Greitemeyer, Tobias, and Silvia Osswald. "Prosocial video games reduce aggressive cognitions." *ScienceDirect*. 14 Apr. 2009. Web. 08 Nov. 2009.

Ivory, James D., and Sriram Kalyanaraman "Video Games Make People Violent—Well, Maybe Not That Game: Effects of Content and Person Abstraction on Perceptions of Violent Video Games' Effects and Support of Censorship." *Communication Reports* 22.1 (2009): 1–12. *Academic Search Elite*. EBSCO. Web. 11 Nov. 2009.

Kohler, Chris. "Videogame Makers Propose Ratings Board to Congress. *Wired News*. 29 July 1994. Web. 23 Nov. 2009.

"Most kids 'unaffected' by violent games." *Sydney Morning Herald*. 1 Apr. 2007. Web. 23 Nov. 2009.

"Parents recognize ESRB ratings, maybe ignore." *Siliconera*. 5 Dec. 2006. Web. 16 Nov. 2009.

"Record Labeling: Transcript of Hearing before United States Senate: First Session on content music and the lyrics of records." *Joe's Apt*. Web. 23 Nov. 2009.

"Undercover Shoppers Find It Increasingly Difficult for Children to Buy M-Rated Games." *Federal Trade Commission*. 8 May 2008. Web. 16 Nov. 2009.

"Violent Video Games Can Increase Aggression." *American Psychological Association*. 23 Apr. 2000. Web. 11 Nov. 2009.

A CLASH OF ELECTRIC BLUE

Nataly Sanchez

Instructor: Dina Abdel Hady

Whether it is a blessing or a curse, technology has influenced our lives as a generation. In this paper, you will choose a specific form of technology and make an argument regarding its effects on society.

My inspiration for this paper was my major: art. I had a hard time writing this paper and had to dedicate extra time writing it. I found myself often upset with my topic, and felt like my writing was going nowhere because of how ardent I was about the subject. I worked really hard on the paper, draft after draft. Overall, I am happy with my paper and the topic I chose. It might have been tough, but it was worth it.

"Write it. Cut it. Paste it. Save it. Load it. Check it. Quick, rewrite it! Surf it. Scroll it. Pause it. Click it. Name it. Rate it. Tune it. Print it." The song "Technologic" by Daft Punk exemplifies the use of technology today. "We live in [such] techno-enthusiastic times," says author Sherry Turkle in her essay "Can You Hear me Now?" that we have become too attached and too dependent on technology (270). Technology has begun to expose different options of viewing and performing tasks even in the field of fine arts by introducing applications and virtual online museums. Art's importance in society is cultural and helps us be more civilized. Because of this, we need to consider technology's effect on it. Not only does technology take away the hands-on experience and beauty of working with mediums, but posting artwork online can also lose the artist's credibility without copyright.

Because programming has allowed users to cut, paste, and edit different media, it has evolved the form of painting and drawing into digital art. For example, Corel Painter is used as an easy way to draw and paint by inexperienced users. Corel Painter is used with a Wacom graphic tablet, which allows the user to use the touch screen and pen to create designs. Corel Painter has turned regular photos into paintings in an unnatural way. The experience does not feel the same as a person who actually paints. Painting is a difficult medium to control, especially watercolor. There are other programs, such as Paintbrush, which have designed a whole new way to 'paint' using computers. Painting means using a brush and paint where paint colors can vary depending on the technique of the brushstrokes. This variation in color cannot be duplicated by programs like Paintbrush because the pixels of color are limited. The program only uses basic concepts of drawing; it does not go into detail nor does it have a hands-on approach as the actual medium. Therefore, the medium and its techniques are not fully appreciated. On some applications, the settings must be changed in order to have different line quality. In drawing or painting, the artist just needs to press down harder or lighter, use thinner pencils and brushes or thicker ones to create different effects. It is faster and has better quality. There is a difference between graphic design and fine art; fine art is a more hands-on experience that is done with pencils, charcoal, and other materials. Computer graphics, on the other hand, use tablets and pens for graphic designs. Although art is being integrated with technology, it does not mean society should switch to its usage and form completely.

Though there may be different programs for fine arts, we cannot always depend on the technology because it can fail us due to the viruses infiltrating it. If the software is not up to date, then there can be viruses and bugs gaining access to the computer's system. When a virus infects the computer, it becomes slow and things begin to malfunction. If one is using a program and something is due the next day and the technology fails, the work cannot be retrieved. On the other hand, a drawing is physically there at one's fingertips. A composition is not going to fail or give any delay. Also, with online artwork such as the online museum, the same things could happen. The art could sometimes not show up, coming up blank, and it can also become expensive. If one signs up for an online art gallery, it is going to cost more than a regular entrance fee. However, some artists prefer online art galleries because through it, they can access all of the artwork that they have in their personal galleries. Also, online galleries are not like regular galleries that only show certain artwork. For example, CSUN's art gallery is free but is limited in its collection. The CSUN art gallery has Robert Williams' artwork on display at the moment, but only until April 2010. Despite this disadvantage, however, at a gallery, one can view the painting or drawing in depth and can feel the texture of the brush strokes or the blending and scrapping of a drawing. This physical connection with art is limited in online galleries because online art reduces the amounts of texture a painting or drawing can have, producing a less enriched composition.

Furthermore, artwork is at the mercy of the Internet due to the artists' inability to control the actions of others stealing their work. Online art can be reproduced tenfold by being able to click it and print it from an online source. The artwork is not appreciated as a real product because the original work loses the true value, depth, size, and texture. For example, artist Julian Beever creates chalk artwork done on sidewalks that are large in scale to create an illusion. His work is two-dimensional, but to the eye, it feels three-dimensional. If a person is looking at his work, it can be viewed in different ways, while through a photograph, it can only be seen through one method, not capturing the artwork as a whole. The printed piece of artwork would feel somewhat flat and result in losing its effect. The different elements to art are what give artwork more significance than just a printed condensed sized of the composition. Because some artworks are available online, it can be viewed by anyone. Even if the composition is deleted, it will always be there no matter what. If someone likes the composition and uses it, they can credit it as their own and say, "Look at my artwork," when in reality they did not construct the piece. There is always someone out there taking credit for someone else's work, whether it is art or even pictures of people. The internet is a whole new way to mask any aspects of the truth, to disguise oneself and lie. It is permanent, and any artwork, if not copyrighted, has the chance of losing creditability for the artist. For example, the site deviantart.com has artwork that varies from traditional artwork to photography. However, the site does not reveal the artist's true name and thus, any artwork on the site can be "stolen" by just dragging it over to the computer's desktop and storing it. It can be reused as someone else's. While artists can sue those who steal their work, it is safer for users to not steal any work in the first place.

Although artwork posted online is more accessible for people, the artists do not get the same feedback that they would from a live audience critiquing their work. People can still comment on the artwork in online forums, but the usual responses are, "Oh, I like it." It does not get discussed as a group and the artwork is less explored. For example, what is its purpose, its significance to the artist, the colors used; not just if it looks perfect, but what does the artwork portray?. It is better to have a live audience than a page of compliments that will most likely not be read after one hundred messages, especially when it becomes repetitive. In a critique, the artist can hear different opinions at once, and discuss the artwork as a whole with another. Technology limits the artist, even on web chat, with the maximum of two other audience members critiquing the work. In an art class, students learn from one another in each critique. If one is praised for one's work, students take notes and try to exemplify their own result using their own technique. The educator is there to help and critique students, while an online discussion could turn into chaos. Yes, there are online tutorials, but can those instructors respond to your questions and work? No, because art is about learning your environment and surroundings.

However, artwork being available online does have some positive effects. Online, art is accessible to a broader range of people who do not have the time to go to galleries. It "will soon be just a mouse-click away," comments Janese Heavin from *Columbia Daily Tribune* on how the State Historical Society of Missouri will be producing an online version of their gallery with over thousands of works. Also, online art helps professors view their students' work in entirety instead of through a massive portfolio. For example, deviantart.com can be used for displaying students' artwork from previous courses or artwork done for enjoyment. This site is also a great way to discover new artists around the world. Of course, it must be considered that in the 1870s, society did not need to find artists the way we do today. Claude Monet did just fine without the Internet and is still a well-known artist even nowadays. The internet has made accessibility to art and the discovery of artists easier; however, the problems it presents outweigh the advantages. Problems such as a limited way of viewing the art or crediting the wrong artist for the piece are more frequent due to technology.

While there may be a couple positive aspects of online art, they are limited. The way art is produced is amazing. It takes hard work and passion. An artist's artwork is precious and should not be confined to a small-digitalized screen because, by doing so, we would be reducing its significance and quality. Art has been a part of society for a long time, progressing each century, and it has not used technology in the past but still managed to continue to strive. So why now?

Works Cited

Daft Punk. "Technologic." *Human After All*. Virgin, 2005. Digital File.

"Digital Painting Fundamental with Corel Painter II." *Reference & Research Book News* (2009). *General OneFile*. Web. 24 February 2010.

"Project to Put History Online: Art, Recordings to be Digitized." *Columbia Daily Tribune* [Columbia, MO]. (2010). *General OneFile*. Web. 24 February 2010.

Turkle, Sherry. "Can You Hear Me Now?" *They Say/I Say: With Readings*. Eds. Cathy Birkenstein, Russel Durst, and Gerald Graff. New York: Norton and Company, 2009. Print.

Wiley, Jennifer Dulin. "The Changing Role of the Art Gallery." *Art Business News* 35.10 (2008). *General OneFile*. Web. 24 February 2010.